Readers Theatre in the Classroom

Readers Theatre in the Classroom

A Manual for Teachers of Children and Adults

by

Melvin Campbell, Ph.D.
and
JoAnn V. Cleland, Ed.D.

iUniverse, Inc.
New York Lincoln Shanghai

Readers Theatre in the Classroom
A Manual for Teachers of Children and Adults

iUniverse, Inc.

For information address:
iUniverse, Inc.
2021 Pine Lake Road, Suite 100
Lincoln, NE 68512
www.iuniverse.com

ISBN: 0-595-30440-0

Printed in the United States of America

Contents

A Few Words to Our Readers

BRIEF HISTORY OF READERS THEATRE

Readers Theatre (RT) dates back to the early 1800s when it was a pastime for literate members of society. Gathered around a table, participants would read Shakespearean plays and other classics, while those in an outer circle of chairs listened. Over time, it seems RT became lost as an art form, until it was used on Broadway for a play called *Don Juan from Hell*. Since that time the RT format has appeared in a variety of settings: weddings, farewell parties, dedications, etc. Many television news broadcasts are in RT style. As two or more individuals read from a TelePrompTer, they do not make eye contact with one another, but look directly at the camera. Usually their sentences are short, and they take turns reading lines; thus they utilize two key features of RT.

Readers Theatre has many venues, but perhaps its most powerful use occurs in instructional settings. On college campuses, 20% of presentations are in RT structure (White and Coger 1967). Its popularity is undoubtedly due to its simple yet effective format, making it a perfect fit to the classroom.

WHY A BOOK ON READERS THEATRE

This book is the result of requests from teachers in schools and students in our courses, who have seen our demonstrations and participated in our professional presentations at conferences for organizations like the International Reading Association and the National Science Teachers Association. These in-service and pre-service teachers have sensed the power, usefulness, and fun of RT; the lights have come on, but teachers are still a bit in the dark about implementation. Their comments have confirmed the need for a book such as this, which attempts to move a good idea into practical application. We hope you will catch the excitement of using RT, not as an add-on, but as a strategy that teaches, reinforces, and reviews instructional content in a quick and motivational way. This book shares our story concerning RT and how it has helped to turn "the lights on" in many students.

ACKNOWLEDGEMENTS

We wish to thank these teachers who have let the joy of RT into their classrooms and given us feedback through the years: Janis Smith, Joyce Cristophal, Nancy Harlan, VirLynn Burton, Mike Irvin, Mary Bragg, Becky Brecher, and Cathy Bowman from the United States; Don Roy, Christine Goad, and Sandra England from Australia; June Peters and Terry Carey from Canada; Jillian Thiele and Peter Iga from Papua New Guinea; Carol Bradfield from the Solomon Islands; Julie Weslake from New Zealand, just to name just a few.

CONTACT INFORMATION

We do workshops and seminars for schools and school districts. You can contact us at mdcamp@dslextreme.com or jvcleland@aol.com.

Melvin Campbell, Ph.D.   JoAnn V. Cleland, Ed.D.

Riverside, California   Phoenix, Arizona

I

Readers Theatre in the Classroom

1

Readers Theatre as an Art Form

SIMPLICITY OF READERS THEATRE

At first glance, the idea of Readers Theatre (RT) seems almost too simple to be viewed as bona fide art. It is just two or more readers voicing words to interpret a variety of literary genre: stories, poems, letters, factual accounts, historical documents, etc. But it is more than merely taking turns reading lines. Every word must contribute to the message. There is an interactivneness to the use of language—with playfulness at times and, at other times, with seriousness and intensity. Readers Theatre requires focusing on the script, concentrating on interpretation, and attending to articulation during the presentation.

PURPOSE OF READERS THEATRE

We have chosen to write Readers Theatre without the apostrophe in the word 'Readers.' The theatre does not belong to the readers. The stage of the theatre is in the minds of the audience as well as the readers. It is on this stage that we want to create battles in social studies, intrigue in literature, wonder in science, and conceptualization in mathematics. Readers Theatre is similar to old-time radio in which listeners were enthralled as they conjured up scenes in their minds while the performers acted only with their voices. This dynamic, that held millions to radio speakers each evening, can also engage your students in the art of reading and listening. Teachers worry that they cannot compete with television, and this is certainly true if we try to utilize TV producers' techniques. But we have advantages over TV. We are alive in the classroom—or at least we should be! Students can be active participants. They can express their emotions through voice tone and natural gestures. The struggles to captivate youths' minds do not belong to TV producers (or to movie directors), but to teachers who can stir the imagination through participatory drama in the form of RT.

UNIQUE CHARACTERISTICS OF READERS THEATRE

The simplicity of RT is best demonstrated through a comparison with plays, operas, television series, and movies. Dramatic forms span a continuum from presentational to representational.

Representational   Presentational

Readers Theatre, in its simplest form, is a verbal presentation with no props, costuming, staging, or choreography—just acting with the voice. This makes it an attractive choice for the classroom. Whether the school is in a high or low socioeconomic area is immaterial, since there is no expense involved. In contrast, representational drama requires sets, costumes, lighting, and extensive rehearsal time. In order to prepare such a performance, a school must be prepared to commit resources, both in money and time.

The most significant difference between representational and presentational drama is the focus. During a representational drama, members of the audience are observers, as actors on stage interact with one another to portray the scenes. They are spectators of a performance with an on-stage focus. Presentational drama, i.e., Readers Theatre, uses an off-stage focus. The scenes unfold in the minds of the audience. The focus of each format determines the other features of these two types of drama. The following chart identifies the characteristics that distinguish representational from presentational styles.

CHARACTERISTICS OF REPRESENTATIONAL AND PRESENTATIONAL THEATRE

Representational Theatre	Presentational Theatre
Play format	Literature adapted or generated for reading only
Actors who assume identities of specific roles	Lines assigned for effect, not necessarily with distinct roles, i.e., some roles taken by multiple readers and some readers assuming multiple roles
On-stage focus Interactions among actors who speak to and look at one another	Off-stage focus No eye contact among readers, who speak and look toward the audience
Overt, purposeful movements to carry action	Only symbolic or natural movement normally associated with expressive reading
Memorized lines; no scripts	Scripts for read lines
Theatre stage as a pictorial environment for the message Costumes, props, scenery, lighting, sound effects, etc.	Theatre environment incidental to the message Little to no costuming or props
Illusion of reality, which the audience is expected to believe	Perception of reality, a creation of each audience member's mind
Audience as spectators	Audience as participants at times

Following is part of a script. As you read it, picture its performance in both representational (play) and presentational (RT) styles.
(See the complete reproducible script in Chapter 12.)

Colonists and Tea Time

6 Readers: CARL, COLIN THE COLONIST, TOM THE TAX COLLECTOR, KING'S REP 1 & 2, KING

CARL: What?
COLIN: New Taxes?
TOM: You got that right.

CARL: I can't believe this.

COLIN: Here is the bill; seeing is believing.

CARL: The King has some nerve.

TOM: The King is King. What can I say?

CARL: We have lived on this continent, how many years now?

TOM: Listen in to this conversation and maybe you will pay your taxes.

…

KING'S REP 2: O King, we are broke!

KING: Broke…as in no money?

KING'S REP 1: The French and Indian War have depleted our funds.

KING'S REP 2: We got a lot of land

…

KING: Excellent! Parliament, pass new taxes.

KING'S REP 1: At your command, oh, King.

KING: They can help refill our treasury.

KING'S REP 2: It is their war that put us in this predicament in the first place.

KING: Tax their tea!

KING'S REP 2: But…

KING'S REP 1: but what if they switch to coffee drinking?

KING: Tax the tea and then the coffee if we have to.

CARL: I have an idea.

COLIN: Let's have a tea party in Boston.

A FINAL WORD

In representational drama, a play, the three men on stage would engage in a heated argument among themselves aboard a ship in the harbor. The actors would look at each other and make appropriate gestures to emphasize their memorized words. Scenery, costumes, and props would provide a colonial setting; house lights would be dimmed to keep the focus on stage.

In presentational drama, a RT, the three would also engage in animated dialogue, but there would be no props, costumes, or exaggerated movements. The readers would look, not at one another, but toward the audience, although without direct eye contact. Holding scripts, they would act with their voices only. Either genre would be effective in the classroom. Each style requires that those portraying the roles have clear understanding of the message. Readers Theatre is just simpler to produce and more likely to stimulate personal imaging within the minds of the readers and the audience.

2

Benefits of Readers Theatre as an Instructional Vehicle

MULTIPLE BENEFITS OF READERS THEATRE

Why use Readers Theatre (RT) in the classroom? The first and foremost reason undoubtedly is getting kids to read and to focus on meaning. Acting with the voice in this straightforward format intensifies attention to comprehension. For many teachers, this is the sole rationale for using RT: a motivational means of enhancing understanding. But, while this is indeed its obvious benefit, RT can provide much more if it is used as a consolidating force rather than an add-on to the curriculum. It can maximize time by simultaneously addressing:

- academic standards,
- transdisciplinary integration,
- the seven basic multiple intelligences, and
- the emotional impetus needed for igniting the learning process.

ACADEMIC STANDARDS

Readers Theatre can be used to address academic standards in any and all subject areas. This book includes examples of scripts for language arts, science/health, mathematics and social studies. The examples in Chapter 9-12 address broad learner outcomes based on national standards in these four core content areas. It should be noted, however, that art, music, physical education, career awareness or any course of study can be enriched through this communication medium. Well-designed use of RT has ubiquitous instructional value.

TRANSDISCIPLINARY INTEGRATION

For virtually every example in this book, standards in more than one discipline can be met. These linkages during RT presentations can serve as catalysts for transdisciplinary integration. During instruction on curriculum development for pre- and in-service teachers, we have seen the amazed looks on their faces when they realize that a RT presentation can anchor an entire thematic unit, setting the stage for instruction in all four basic disciplines. Well-designed use of RT has powerful connective potential.

MULTIPLE INTELLIGENCES

Readers Theatre is a natural companion to the multiple intelligences theory Gardner (1983). We have observed many "aha!" moments as teachers construct instructional plans centered on RT. Without even intending to do so, the teacher who writes a lesson plan centered on a RT, automatically includes stimulation of verbal/linguistic, logical/mathematical, visual/spatial, musical/rhythmic, interpersonal, and intrapersonal intelligences. Every child can find a comfort zone in at least one of these domains, thereby internalizing the concept of the day through his/her strongest learning channel. Well-designed use of RT has avenues for reaching each student through her favored learning style.

EMOTIONAL CONCERNS

Research shows that emotion strongly influences the learner's receptivity, assimilation, and retention. Readers Theatre, if appropriately implemented, provides "relaxed alertness" (Caine 1991). That is, attention is heightened but without fear of failure. Few instructional strategies provide such a stimulating but safe climate as well as Readers Theatre. Well-designed use of RT has the capacity to touch the soul with a warming flame. The impact on students' emotions is well documented for shy children with special needs, who require a different modality of expression (Martinez 1999).

RATIONALE FOR USE

Readers Theatre is a powerful instructional tool to teach academics, link subject areas, open a range of learning avenues, and provide a supportive social and emotional classroom climate.

The following is a list of reasons for using RT with students, enumerating not only its academic and social values, but also its practicality for teachers (Roy 2000). Readers Theatre:

- develops literacy.

- makes students eager to read.

- encourages students to read original literature.

- engages students in thinking while they are reading.

- provides exposure to and focuses on literary forms and techniques: imagery, metaphors, idioms, and structures of specific genre.

- encourages expressive reading.

- provides for dramatic interpretation and production.

- provides opportunity for role-taking.

- allows for dramatic presentation with minimal staging.

- focuses and holds attention.

- calls for sensitivity and cooperation.

- provides a vehicle for teaching content material.

- is adaptable to groups of various sizes, ages, and abilities.

- affirms reading competence in strong readers.

- builds self-confidence, particularly for struggling readers.

BENEFITS TO STRUGGLING AND SECOND LANGUAGE READERS

Prescott (2003) shares anecdotal accounts on the value of RT. In one classroom, after just ten weeks' use of RT, every student's reading level increased by one grade. Prescott relates dramatic successes with 3rd, 4th, and 6th grade students using RT.

A scientific study (Martinez 1999) shows clear improvement among 2nd grade students who consistently used RT as a part of the reading program. The areas of improvement were fluidity, phrasing, and expressiveness of oral reading. In their concluding remarks the researchers state, "Readers Theatre seems to offer teachers a way to incorporate repeated readings within a meaningful and purposeful context."

All can succeed at RT! Script structure, role assignments, and delivery style can be subtly manipulated to scaffold for struggling readers without reducing the challenges for more capable readers, or "dumbing down" any part of the presentation.

Script structure is an important part of helping struggling readers. To ensure that less-experienced readers feel successful and fully engaged, we have chosen to write scripts with short lines, often single words. This reduces the within-line load for the struggling readers. We also random-order voice entries, requiring every participant to attend to reading throughout the presentation. Inexperienced readers have reason to be making voice-print match as they follow others' lines while looking for their own.

Role Assignments can provide success to the struggling reader. Often the shortest lines have dynamic impact. When these power-packed words are assigned to struggling readers, it increases their need to read expressively and their sense of contribution to the message. Frequently, the struggling readers are the "show-stoppers!" What a confidence-builder for those who usually find reading time boring or embarrassing!

Delivery style can actually enhance the struggling readers use of the language. The neurological impress method (Hecklemann 1969) is a rather simple technique effective in helping children with severe reading disabilities. A fluent reader reads directly into the ear of a less competent reader, who joins the expressive flow provided by his peer. Normally, errors are not corrected so as not to interrupt meaning or the cadence of the language. We sometimes apply this technique to RT. Here's how it works. Two students, a good reader and a struggling reader, are assigned the same part. The weaker reader holds the script to ensure her close attention to text. The stronger reader stands directly behind her. As he reads over her shoulder, she joins in the flow of language, making voice-print matches without the pressure of a solo performance. It is essential that the less capable reader not feel singled out. To avoid the possibility of such identification, we recommend making many role pairs, mixing reading abilities to prevent labeling. There are advantages to this procedure for everyone. The struggling reader is still part of the class, enjoying the dynamics of the experience, but she suffers no stigma. The more capable reader intuitively senses the need to model accuracy and expressiveness, but does not lose any learning time to provide coaching.

Even non-readers can become viable members of the RT troupe. LEP (limited English proficient) learners can be assigned to lines that contain repetition and are chorally read. They follow the pattern and are pulled into the cadence set by their peers. These chorally read lines may be assigned to a small group or to the whole class, but should make strong contributions to the message of the selection.

A SPECIFIC EXAMPLE

In the following example, note the opportunity for Reader 5 to "catch on" and join in after participating in reading three times in the "All Readers Group" before he/she reads the line alone.
(See the complete reproducible script in Chapter 10.)

Implementation of the Zebra Reader Theatre

In this example, Reader 5 is engaged from the first line to the last, but is constantly supported. He has one solo line, but need only echo the words of the group.

The teacher who chooses or writes RT with differentiated roles, assigns parts carefully, and provides inconspicuous support for struggling readers is drawing the less-experienced readers into the community of learners. At the same time she is increasing word power and comprehension for all students.

It was intriguing to note, during the presentation of a RT in a third grade classroom, that the poor oral readers actually read their lines with better expression than the traditional "good" readers. What a source of encouragement for these struggling readers. In an eleventh-grade American literature class students were to write their own RT scripts, interpreting the selection of literature assigned. A student, whom the regular teacher described as just barely passing, prepared by far the best script. It appeared that learning was occurring for this student; she simply needed a different manner to exhibit it!

The Zebra

5 Readers

ALL READERS: The zebra, the zebra, the zebra
READER 1: has such a funny hide.
ALL READERS: The zebra, the zebra, the zebra—
READER 3: We never can decide
READER 4: whether he's white
READER 2: with stripes of black,
READER 3: or black
READER 2: with stripes of white.
ALL READERS: Oh, zebra,
READER 5: oh, zebra, oh, zebra,
READER 3: oh, tell us which is right—
READER 4: white stripes on black
ALL READERS: or black stripes on white?

A FINAL WORD

Our experience indicates that RT provides a number of benefits to teachers, some obvious and others subtler. The combination of developing literacy while at the same time teaching the content material is a must for today's teachers; there is growing pressure on educators to generate good readers as well as students who know content. Through RT the teacher can make the material relevant to the students, while maximizing their participation. Many students who are reluctant to participate in class find this teaching strategy engaging and fun. Finally the great benefit to the teacher is that the use of RT is not an add-on to instruction but an integral part of it.

II

Readers Theatre Scripts

3

Arranging Texts for Readers Theatre

TYPES OF READERS THEATRE SCRIPTS

There is no one-way to write a Readers Theatre (RT) script. As with any art form its structure will be determined by what the writer envisions as the final product of presentation, keeping in mind the needs and interests of the audience, but, most important, of the readers. For our purposes, we see students in the classroom learning content and developing the ability to read via RT scripts. Superimposed on all of this is the age level of the student. What is suitable for one age group may not be appropriate for another. For our purposes we will discuss and give examples of four types of RT scripts we have found especially well suited for the classroom:

    A. simple presentation

    B. storytelling with dialogue

    C. readings with echo responses

    D. reading with audience as a character

USE OF FOLKLORE

Many of the scripts in this collection are based on folklore, i.e. nursery rhymes, fairy tales, fables, etc. The purpose for these choices is two-fold: to launch students' experiences with RT from a familiar base; and to raise teachers' confi-

dence in their ability to create engaging learning opportunities through this
simple format.

A. SIMPLE PRESENTATION

A simple presentational RT is used to tell a story with the readers' lines
assigned in random fashion. Typically no dialogue is used and when it is a part
of the story no one reader is assigned those lines. This is illustrated by the use
of three readers as they tell the familiar nursery rhyme, "Humpty Dumpty."
The readers are designated non-sequentially to ensure that the readers focus
on the script throughout the presentation.

This RT script is much longer than the actual Humpty Dumpty poem.
The first three lines are easily read giving the students confidence in oral reading from the very beginning. The next seventeen lines pull words out of the
poem prefaced by 'This is a poem' line. Lines are purposely repeated to give
added confidence to the oral readers.
(See the complete reproducible script in Chapter 9.)

Humpty Dumpty
3 Readers

READER 1: My last name is _____. I will read the part of Reader One.
READER 2: My last name is _____. I will read the part of Reader Two.
READER 3: My last name is _____. I will read the part of Reader Three.

READER 1: Humpty Dumpty
READER 3: may sound like
READER 1: a silly poem about eggs.
READER 2: It is a poem
READER 3: about walls and falls.
READER 1: It is a poem
READER 2: about horses and men.
READER 1: It is a poem
READER 3: about putting things
READER 2: together again.
READER 3: It is a poem
READER 1: that tells us to be careful where we go,
READER 2: how we sit,

READER 3: and what we do,
READER 2: and how we fall.
READER 1: Here is the poem called
ALL READERS: Humpty Dumpty!

READER 3: Humpty Dumpty
READER 2: sat on a wall,
READER 1: Humpty Dumpty
READER 2: had a great fall:
READER 3: All the King's horses
READER 1: and all the King's men can't put,
READER 3: can't put Humpty Dumpty together again.
READER 2: Poor Humpty Dumpty
ALL READERS: is all cracked up!

B. STORYTELLING WITH DIALOGUE

The script that follows provides an example of an effective way to tell a story with the characters' dialogue lines interspersed throughout the reading. The narrators carry the storyline, the backbone of the reading, which gives support and meaning to the dialogue. The following story adapted for RT is an example of interactions among six characters: Cinderella, two stepsisters, Fairy Godperson, Footman, and Prince.

Implementation of the Cinderella Reader Theatre

There is predictable repetition throughout this reading, but it is not always the same person reading the repeated lines. We therefore maintain the predictable repetition while requiring the readers to focus on the script at all times.

Also note that many of the lines are only two words in length. This technique mirrors how people interact with one another in real life. If you listen to conversations, you will notice that some participants interject only a few words at a time. Storytelling with dialogue should sound like everyday conversation. *(See the complete reproducible script in Chapter 9.)*

Cinderella

8 Readers: NARRATOR 1,2; SISTER 1,2; CINDERELLA, FAIRY GODPERSON,
FOOTMAN, PRINCE

SISTER 1: Cinderella!
SISTER 2: Sweep the floor.
SISTER 1: Cinderella!
SISTER 2: Wash the dishes.
SISTER 1: Cinderella!
SISTER 2: Make the beds.
SISTER 1: Cinderella!
SISTER 2: Clean the windows.

...

SISTER 1: Do this.
SISTER 2: Do that.
CINDERELLA: Yes, and do this and that.
NARRATOR 1: In the afternoon
NARRATOR 2: the stepsisters spent their time trying to make themselves
beautiful.

...

SISTERS 1,2: This is a perfect fit!
NARRATOR 2: The footman had tried everyone in the kingdom
NARRATOR 1: and since the shoe didn't fit
NARRATOR 2: no one was to wear it.
NARRATOR 1: Just then Cinderella walked into the room with mops and
brooms
NARRATOR 2: with buckets and rags,

...

NARRATOR 2: You should be careful how you treat other people
NARRATOR 1: because the shoe you make other people walk in
NARRATOR 2: you may have to wear yourself.
NARRATOR 1: As for Cinderella she liked the old saying—
CINDERELLA: If the shoe fits, wear it!

C. READING WITH ECHO RESPONSES

An easy way to involve the audience is through echo reading. In this style of
RT, the audience repeats the lines read by a voice leader. Typically two or

more narrators tell the story in the script, while a voice leader intersperses lines, which are immediately repeated by the audience.

Originally echo readings were designed to be used in primary school where students either could not read or where English was a second language. Over time, we have learned that echo reading is successful with non-readers and readers alike. It shows the non-readers how much fun written words can be, and helps them experience the correct pronunciation and cadence of the language; simultaneously, all students are learning content. Audiences of every age find it challenging and interesting to imitate a voice leader. Students who can read are attracted to the voice leader part. They love using their voices expressively and having the audience repeat their words. Students assigned to this role have been given a position of leadership and power in the use of words. They love it!

Three Little Kittens, is an example of a RT script in which the audience repeats the words of the Voice Leader.
(See the complete reproducible script in Chapter 9.)

Three Little Kittens
4 Readers: READER 1,2,3; VOICE LEADER

READER 1: One.
READER 2: Two.
READER 3: Three little kittens.
READER 2: Lost their mittens!
READER 1: And they began to cry,
ALL READERS: Oh, Mother dear,
…
VOICE LEADER: You naughty kittens!
READER 1: Meow.
VOICE LEADER: Then, you shall have no pie.
READER 2: Meow.
READER 3: Meow.
VOICE LEADER: MEOW!
READER 3: The one
READER 2: two
…

VOICE LEADER: Then you shall have some pie.
READER 1: Purr.
READER 2: Purr.
READER 3: Purr
VOICE LEADER: Purrrrrr.
READER 1: The end of purring and this story.

"The Old Lady" is another example of interaction between the audience and a small group of solo readers. The Audience is cued by one of the Readers, who, at the appropriate time, holds up a card with the line, 'Perhaps she'll die.' Thus only the readers need copies of the script.
(See the complete reproducible script in Chapter 9.)

Old Lady

5 Readers: READER 1,2,3,4; AUDIENCE

READER 1: There was an old lady who swallowed a fly.
READER 2: I don't know why she swallowed a fly.
AUDIENCE: Perhaps she'll die.
READER 1: There was an old lady who swallowed a spider
READER 3: that wriggled and wriggled and jiggled inside her.
READER 4: She swallowed the spider to catch the fly.
READER 2: I don't know why she swallowed a fly.
…
READER 4: She swallowed the bird to catch the spider,
READER 3: that wriggled and wriggled and jiggled inside her.
READER 4: She swallowed the spider to catch the fly.
READER 2: I don't know why she swallowed a fly.
AUDIENCE: Perhaps she'll die.
READER 1: There was an old lady who swallowed a dog.
READER 2: What a hog, to swallow a dog!
READER 1: She swallowed the dog to catch the cat.
READER 2: She swallowed the cat to catch the bird.
…
READER 4: She swallowed the spider to catch the fly.
READER 2: I don't know why she swallowed a fly.
AUDIENCE: Perhaps she'll die.

READER 1: There was an old lady who swallowed a horse.
AUDIENCE: Perhaps she'll die.
READER 4: Perhaps? Perhaps?
ALL READERS: She's dead!
READER 1: Of course.

D. READING WITH AUDIENCE AS A CHARACTER

Choral reading, like echo reading, gives students the comfort of the group, as they are swept into fluent, expressive performances. Having the audience take part in a reading as one of the characters gives added interest. In the following script the audience, in dialogue with the psychologist, plays the Patient. *(See the complete reproducible script in Chapter 10.)*

How Do You Feel Today?

by Dusty Castro
4 readers: NARRATORS 1,2, PSYCHOLOGIST, PATIENT (AUDIENCE)

NARRATOR 1: Life today is certainly not easy.
NARRATOR 2: Most of us
NARRATOR 1: could use more time
NARRATOR 2: to ourselves.
NARRATOR 1: To be free of the everyday
...
NARRATOR 2: Talking.
NARRATOR 1: About what?
NARRATOR 2: Something like,
PSYCHOLOGIST: How do you feel today?
PATIENT: Disappointed.
PSYCHOLOGIST: Why is that?
PATIENT: No raise from the boss.
PSYCHOLOGIST: You expected it soon?
PATIENT: He said this week.
PSYCHOLOGIST: That is quite a disappointment.
PATIENT: A big one.
PSYCHOLOGIST: Other feelings?
PATIENT: Definitely perplexed.
...

PATIENT: Much relieved.
PSYCHOLOGIST: What an improvement!
PATIENT: Yeh. My luck. I won.
PSYCHOLOGIST: The big money?
PATIENT: Biiiig money!
PSYCHOLOGIST: So we're through.
PATIENT: Seems so.
PSYCHOLOGIST: Perhaps so.
NARRATOR 1: NOT SO!
NARRATOR 2: Is that so?
NARRATOR 1: He'll be back.

A FINAL WORD

The teacher's academic goal should drive the selection of the text and the decision regarding the style of the RT script. A powerful attribute of Readers Theatre is its capacity to engage a community of learners in focused concept development, while providing differentiated assignments to meet the needs of students with a wide range of reading skills. The wise teacher seeks a story or expository work that embodies the content to be learned in a dynamic manner. She then envisions each of her students as she chooses the format: simple presentation, storytelling with dialogue, reading with echo responses, or reading with the audience as a character. She asks herself, "How can I design this experience so every child feels involved but not threatened? How can I lead all my students to grasp this concept in a meaningful, memorable manner?"

4

Rewriting Texts for a Readers Theatre

Occasionally a Readers Theatre (RT) can be found to suit the instructional needs of the classroom, and its use can be very effective. More often there is no script appropriate to a particular learning situation, leaving the teacher with the task of writing the script. This chapter endeavors to provide the teacher with strategies for writing RT scripts in a minimum of time.

STEPS IN PREPARATION OF A READERS THEATRE

- Selecting the Literature
- Preparing the Script
- Editing the Script
- Piloting the Script
- Providing Credits and Disclaimers

Selecting the Literature

Select a story or piece of literature appropriate for the age level in terms of **words, concepts,** and **interests** that support the lesson. Choices are endless. Following are some things to keep in mind.

The content and the reading proficiency of the students will determine which of the four types of RT is most appropriate. It needs to demand attention and have an emotional impact. Remember that emotion is the driving factor in learning and can be influenced by the presentational approach you select.

- simple presentation
- storytelling with dialogue
- reading with echo responses
- audience as a character

The language should have a **cadence** that flows to increase readability and understanding. Metaphors, figures of speech, key phrases, and **vivid words** make the script interesting. If the original text contains a situation that poses a dilemma it will evoke an emotional response on the part of both readers and audience. Good drama has **tension or conflict**.

Familiar works are a good starting place. It is not necessary to use an entire selection. An important step is narrowing to only that which meets instructional needs. Following is a list of many writing forms that can be turned into RT scripts. The list is headed by children's picture books for a very good reason. Many have mature themes encapsulated in a minimum of words and in language easily adapted to the RT format.

- Picture books
- Magazine articles
- News releases
- Speeches by great orators, e.g., Presidents, other historical figures
- Letters of significance
- Poems
- Selected portions of a book
- Recipes
- Song lyrics
- Students' short stories
- Student and faculty handbooks
- Movie scripts

- Plays

If the selection is not well known, it must be sequenced so it is easily understood.

Preparing the Script

Copy the Text

Key the text into a word processor document. Delete any text you deem unessential to the script. (Not every word is useful or wanted.) Put an asterisk before the text that is or will become dialogue. The remainder of the text then will be narration. We rarely retain quotation marks in the final script.

Determine the number and type of roles

Divide the narration. Usually two readers serve as the narrators, who carry the story line, the backbone for the script. More narrators may be included, depending on the story and the need to involve more students. There must be enough lines for every participant to be a reader. This ensures that all students focus on the text.

Rearrange the lines

Determine the number of readers who will be involved in the dialogue. It is effective at times to have two individuals take the part of one person. An example of this is in the RT script of "I Have a Dream," (See Chapter 12).

Sometimes interpreters can be used very effectively to intersperse commentaries throughout a script. The lines of the interpreters or chorus, are not found in the original literature, but as ones the author of the RT script adds to support the goals of the classroom. These lines can serve any of the following functions:

- Echoer of important words, phrases or ideas

- Announcer of important words, phrases or ideas

- The devil's advocate

- The story's cynic

- The story's humorist

- The story's conscience

- Producer of sound effects

- Announcer of introductory and/or concluding remarks

Break the text into short lines. Divide the text so that each reader will, in general, read no more than ten words. This means that sentences will often be divided among readers. Where this occurs will depend on the literature selection, but, however it is divided, the text must maintain a smooth flow of language. Assigning short lines facilitates the basic characteristic of Readers Theatre—acting with the voice.

Use the replace function on the word processor to change the numbers to the names of the readers. For example, all the "1's" become "Reader 1," etc. Format the script in a readable fashion.

Editing the Script

Make the final editing touches. Careful use of punctuation marks will help the readers interpret their lines.

Piloting the Script

If possible have a read-through before using the script. Just asking two people to read every other line will give you, the writer, a good idea of flow and rhythm, as well as the level of interest the script creates. Make changes as needed and you are ready to use the script.

Providing Credits and Disclaimers

Be sure to give credit to the author of the original literature on the final version of the script. Preserve the integrity of the original selection. If you have changed the original wording to arouse interest, add a disclaimer stating that the original selection has been "adapted for Readers Theatre."

EXAMPLES OF WRITING THE FOUR TYPES OF READERS THEATRE SCRIPTS

The following examples show the process of writing scripts for the four basic types of Readers Theatres:

- simple presentation
- storytelling with dialogue
- reading with echo responses
- audience as a character

RT as Simple Presentational—The Gettysburg Address

Copy the Text

The Text for this example, The Gettysburg Address, was found on the Internet, copied and pasted into this document. This saved keying in the text.

> Fourscore and seven years ago our fathers brought forth on this continent a new nation, conceived in liberty and dedicated to the proposition that all men are created equal. Now we are engaged in a great civil war, testing whether that nation or any nation so conceived and so dedicated can long endure. We are met on a great battlefield of that war. We have come to dedicate a portion of that field as a final resting place for those who here gave their lives that that nation might live. It is altogether fitting and proper that we should do this. But in larger sense, we cannot dedicate, we cannot consecrate, we cannot hallow this ground. The brave men, living and dead who struggled here have consecrated it far above our poor power to add or detract. The world will little note nor long remember what we say here, but it can never forget what they did here. It is for us the living rather to be dedicated here to the unfinished work, which they who fought here have thus far so nobly advanced. It is rather for us to be here dedicated to the great task remaining before us that from these honored dead we take increased devotion to that cause for which they gave the last full measure of devotion that we here highly resolve that these dead shall not have died in vain, that this nation under God shall have a new birth of freedom, and that government of the people, by the people, for the people shall not perish from the earth.

Determine the numbers and types of roles

We chose to prepare this famous speech as a simple presentational RT for four voices. We felt that the wording of the address was so well crafted that it would be an injustice to Lincoln to make any changes to the original text.

Rearrange the lines

The address was divided and numbers assigned so each reader has separate lines to read. The randomness of the reader order adds interest to the performance and requires that all readers focus on the text throughout the presentation.

1 Fourscore and seven years ago
2 our fathers
3 brought forth on this continent a new nation,
4 conceived in liberty
2 and dedicated to the proposition
3 that all men are created equal.
1 Now we are engaged in a great civil war,
4 testing whether that nation
3 or any nation
4 so conceived
1 and so dedicated can long endure.
2 We are met on a great battlefield of that war.
4 We have come to dedicate a portion of that field
3 as a final resting-place
1 for those who here gave their lives
2 that that nation might live.
3 It is altogether fitting
4 and proper that we should do this.
1 But in a larger sense,
3 we cannot dedicate,
2 we cannot consecrate,
4 we cannot hallow this ground.
2 The brave men,
3 living and dead
1 who struggled here

4 have consecrated it far above
2 our poor power to add or detract.
3 The world will little note
2 nor long remember what we say here,
1 but it can never forget
4 what they did here.
2 It is for us the living
4 rather to be dedicated here to the unfinished work
2 which they who fought here
3 have thus far so nobly advanced.
4 It is rather for us
1 to be here dedicated to the great task remaining before us—
2 that from these honored dead
3 we take increased devotion
4 to that cause for which they gave the last full measure of devotion—
2 that we here highly resolve
1 that these dead
3 shall not have died in vain,
4 that this nation under God
1 shall have a new birth of freedom,
2 and that government
4 of the people,
3 by the people,
1 for the people
4 shall not perish from the earth.

The numbers were next changed to reader names through use of the replacement function—in this case, Reader 1:, Reader 2: etc. To enhance the meaning, various combinations of readers were assigned.

The script was edited, piloted and slightly modified. Within an hour's time, this simple presentational script of Lincoln's famous address was ready for use. Performance of this RT requires no props or costumes, just the voices of four people reading expressively.
(See the complete reproducible script in Chapter 12.)

Gettysburg Address
By Abraham Lincoln adapted for Readers Theatre
4 Readers

READER 1: Fourscore and seven years ago
READER 2: our fathers
READER 3: brought forth on this continent a new nation,
READER 4: conceived in liberty
READER 2: and dedicated to the proposition
READER 3: that all men are created equal.

…

READER 1: for those who here gave their lives
READER 2: that that nation might live.
READER 3: It is altogether fitting
READER 4: and proper that we should do this.

…

READER 4: have consecrated it far above
READER 2: our poor power to add or detract.
READER 3: The world will little note
READER 2: nor long remember what we say here,
READER 1: but it can never forget
READER 4: what they did here.

…

READER 3: shall not have died in vain,
READER 4: that this nation under God
READER 1: shall have a new birth of freedom,
READER 2: and that government
READER 4: of the people,
READER 3: by the people,
READER 1: for the people
READER 4: shall not perish from the earth.

RT as Simple Presentational—"If All the Seas were One Sea"

Many find that poetry is the easiest writing form to adapt for RT, because a poet is careful to make line breaks that dictate how the piece should sound when read orally. Converting this poem to a RT for four readers gives additional life to the written words and prevents the singsong presentation often resulting from a solo voice or full-class choral reading.

Copy the text

Like many poems, "If All the Seas were One Sea," by an anonymous author, is short and therefore easy to key into a document.

> If all the seas were one sea,
> What a great sea that would be!
> If all the trees were one tree,
> What a great tree that would be!
> And if all the axes were one axe,
> What a great axe that would be!
> And if all the men were one man,
> What a great man that would be!
> And if the great man took the great axe,
> And cut down the great tree,
> And let it fall into the great sea,
> What a splish-splash that would be!

Determine the number and types of roles

As with most poetry, no rewording was advisable. We simply divided lines among five readers/reading groups.

Rearrange the lines

Numbers were assigned to the lines throughout the script in a random fashion.

1 If all the seas were one sea,
3 what a great sea,
5 that would be!
2 If all the trees were one tree,
4 what a great tree,
5 that would be!

1 And if all the axes were one axe,
4 what a great axe,
5 that would be!
2 And if all the men were one man,
3 what a great man,
5 that would be!
1 And if the great man
2 took the great axe,
1 and cut down the great tree,
2 and let it fall into the great sea,
4 what a splish-splash,
5 that would be!

The replacement function was used to convert the numbers to reader labels. The script was edited and piloted. During this process, we decided on an adjustment. We reduce the five roles to four, giving lines originally marked as Reader 5 to Reader 3 and 4. This established an effect pattern: Readers 1 and 2 introduce the lines, and Readers 3 and 4 respond, ending each of their responses with a powerful repetition.

If All the Seas Were One Sea

Anonymous
4 Readers

READER 1: If all the seas were one sea,
READER 3: what a great sea,
READER 3,4: that would be!
READER 2: If all the trees were one tree,
READER 4: what a great tree,
READER 3,4: that would be!
READER 1: And if all the axes were one axe,
READER 4: what a great axe,
READER 3,4: that would be!
READER 2: And if all the men were one man,
READER 3: what a great man,
READER 3,4: that would be!
READER 1: And if the great man
READER 2: took the great axe,

READER 1: and cut down the great tree,
READER 2: and let it fall into the great sea,
READER 4: what a splish-splash,
READER 3,4: that would be!

RT as Simple Presentational—Goldilocks

Copy the text

Of the many versions of the Goldilocks, the following one was selected for this script.

Once upon a time there were three bears, papa, mama, and baby. They lived in a small cottage in the middle of the woods. Every morning Mama Bear would fix breakfast of oatmeal for the family. One morning she made the oatmeal so hot that Papa Bear suggested a little walk so the oatmeal could cool. The three bears were off in the fresh morning air, but they forgot to close and lock the door behind them. Goldilocks was also out that very morning. She soon came upon the bears' cottage. Since the door was open she peeped inside and asked if anyone was home. She saw the oatmeal on the table and decided to eat one bowl since no one would know. When she saw the three bowls she tasted the first big bowl and found it to be too salty. The middle-sized bowl turned out to be too sweet. She didn't like either one of them. Then she tasted the oatmeal from the smallest bowl and it was just right. So she ate it all. She saw the three chairs by the fireplace so she decided to rest a while. The first chair was big enough for her but too hard. The middle-sized chair turned out to be too soft. It was the little chair that was very comfortable and just right. She was far too heavy for the little chair and it broke into a dozen pieces on the floor. Goldilocks saw the stairs going upstairs, so she thought she would explore a bit. Upstairs were the beds. She tried the big bed and it was too hard. She tried the middle-sized bed and it was too soft. But the little bed was just right so she fell asleep. She slept so soundly that she didn't hear the bears come home. They too were hungry and tired from their walk. It didn't take long for the bears to notice something was wrong. Baby bear said that someone has eaten all his oatmeal. It looked to the Papa and Mama Bear that someone had tasted their oatmeal as well. The bears then noticed that something was wrong with the chairs by the fireplace. Sure enough Papa and Mama Bears noticed that someone had been sitting in their chairs. Then Baby Bear saw that his chair was broken into a dozen pieces on the floor. He cried and cried. By now the bears were very angry. So they went upstairs and Papa and Mama Bear saw that someone had been in their beds. Baby Bear noticed that some one had not only been in his bed, but someone was in his bed right now. By now the bears had made so much noise so that Goldilocks was awakened. She was so scared that she jumped up from the bed, ran down the stairs and out of the cottage. And she never came back. As for the bears they always locked their doors when going for a walk.

Determine the number and types of roles

The Goldilocks text was divided into shorter lines to be read by six people: two narrators, Goldilocks, and the three bears. The narrators carry the storyline with Goldilocks and the bears responding to them.

Rearrange the text

While the essence of the story is kept throughout the script some changes were made to increase interest. Note the following alterations to the story:

- The text was broken so the number of words per line did not exceed ten.

- Some of the descriptive text was changed to dialogue.

- Some lines were added to heighten the message.

- Phrases and lines were repeated for emphasis.

- Parts of the text were rewritten and/or removed.

Once the text was divided, Narrators 1 and 2, Papa Bear, Mama Bear, Baby Bear and Goldilocks were given numbers 1-6 respectively and assigned to the appropriate lines. The numbers were then changed to the names of the readers with the replacement function on the computer. The script was formatted, edited, piloted and put into final form.
(See the complete reproducible script in Chapter 9.)

Goldilocks and the Three Bears

6 Readers: NARRATORS 1, 2; PAPA BEAR, MAMMA BEAR, BABY BEAR, GOLDILOCKS

NARRATOR 1: Once there were three bears

NARRATOR 2: who had three gruff voices.
NARRATOR 1: The Papa Bear sounded like this—
PAPA BEAR: Loud gruff voice!
NARRATOR 2: Mamma Bear sounded like this—
MAMA BEAR: Soft gruff voice!
NARRATOR 1: And the little Baby Bear sounded like this—
BABY BEAR: Tiny gruff voice!
NARRATOR 2: When the three bears talked to one another they spoke in a—

...

NARRATOR 1: Sitting may be for bears
NARRATOR 2: but not for the likes of Goldilocks;
NARRATOR 1: because even though she was a jogger
NARRATOR 2: she was just too heavy for the chair,
NARRATOR 1: and it broke in pieces!
NARRATOR 2: Goldilocks was heavier than Baby Bear!
GOLDILOCKS: They don't make things like they used to.
NARRATOR 1: Goldilocks picked herself up
NARRATOR 2: and went up the stairs to the bedrooms.

...

NARRATOR 1: Once inside Baby Bear said
NARRATOR 2: in his tiny gruff voice,
BABY BEAR: Someone has eaten my oatmeal!
NARRATOR 1: The reason of course was that
GOLDILOCKS: it tasted just right!
NARRATOR 1: Papa Bear looked at his oatmeal and said in his loud gruff voice,
PAPA BEAR: No one ate mine,
NARRATOR 2: which was true because
GOLDILOCKS: it tasted too salty!
NARRATOR 1: Mamma Bear looked at her oatmeal and said in a soft gruff voice,

...

NARRATOR 2: Close behind her were the three bears
NARRATOR 1: trying to catch her and shouting in their gruffest voices,
ALL BEARS: Who are you? What do you want?
NARRATOR 1: But since Goldilocks had her breakfast of oatmeal and a good nap,
NARRATOR 2: she easily outran the bears.

NARRATOR 1: Here is one conclusion to this story.
NARRATOR 2: Jogging,
NARRATOR 1: depending on where you jog,
NARRATOR 2: may be dangerous to your health!

RT with Echo Response—Little Miss Muffet

Copy the text

A good starting point for a novice at writing Readers Theatre scripts is simply keying in a nursery rhyme.

> Little Miss Muffet
> Sat on a tuffet
> Eating her curds and whey.
> Along came a spider
> And sat down beside her
> And frightened Miss Muffet away.

Determine the number and types of roles

In order to help young readers match sound to print, we decided to use the echo-response style. This short poem is ideal for two solo narrators and a Voice Leader, whose lines are echoed by the audience.

Rearrange the lines

We added introductory lines for the Voice Leader, making following directions part of the performance. We decided to increase the number of times children would read the same words by repeating lines as both statements and questions. (What a subtle way to reinforce declarative and interrogative sentence structures!) The remaining lines were assigned to the two narrators. Children given the roles of narrators always feel honored, but note that the most interesting lines are given to the audience, thus drawing less capable readers into animated choral reading. Finally the text was edited and piloted.

Implementation of an Echo Script

An echo response script has the advantage that only the Narrators and Voice Leader need the script. The Voice Leader reads one line at a time and waits for the audience to imitate her words along with the volume and intonation of her voice.

Little Miss Muffet

3 Readers: NARRATORS 1 & 2, VOICE LEADER

NARRATOR 1: My name is _____. I will be NARRATOR 1.
NARRATOR 2: My name is _____. I will be NARRATOR 2.
VOICE LEADER: My name is _____. I will be your fearless voice leader.
Whatever I say, you will repeat after me. Let's practice that a little.
Voice Leader reads one line at a time and then waits for audience response.
Say it again.
exasperated
That's it?
That's it.
OK!
Sigh, sigh, sigh.

NARRATOR: And now—
VOICE LEADER:
The poem
Little Miss Muffet.

NARRATOR 1: Little Miss Muffet
NARRATOR 2: sat on a tuffet
VOICE LEADER:
eating her curds and whey?
eating her curds and whey.
Yuk! Yuk! Yuk!

NARRATOR 1: Along came a spider
NARRATOR 2: and sat down beside her and

VOICE LEADER:
frightened Miss Muffet away?
Yes,
frightened Miss Muffet away.

NARRATOR 1: EEK!
NARRATOR 2: Who wants these yucky curds and whey?
VOICE LEADER:
Not I.
Nor I.
The End of Miss Muffet.

RT with Audience as Character—Three Billy Goats Gruff.

Copy the text

Folk tales are another excellent source for RT scripts, because you can adjust the length, vocabulary level, and sentence style to meet the needs of your students—without qualms. We keyed in this version of "The Three Billy Goats Gruff."

Once upon a time, there were three billy goats, a little goat, a middle goat, and a big goat. They had eaten all the grass in the field, and they were hungry. They could see green grass on the other side of the river, so they wanted to cross the bridge. Little Goat started across the bridge. Trip, trap, trip, trap, trip, trap. Suddenly a troll came up out of the water. He roared, "Who's that trip-trapping on my bridge!?" Little Goat answered in a shaky voice, "It is I, Little Goat." The troll shouted, "Get off my bridge or I will eat you!" Little Goat replied, "Oh, please do not eat me. My bigger brother is coming. You will like him better." The troll growled, but he let Little Goat pass over the bridge. Next Middle Goat started across the bridge. Trip, trap, trip, trap, trip, trap. Suddenly the troll came up out of the water. He roared, "Who's that trip-trapping on my bridge!?" Middle Goat answered in a shaky voice, "It is I, Middle Goat." The troll shouted, "Get off my bridge or I will eat you!" Middle Goat replied, "Oh, please do not eat me. My bigger brother is coming. You will like him better." The troll growled, but he let Middle Goat pass over the bridge. Big Goat started across the bridge. Trip, trap, trip, trap, trip, trap. Suddenly the troll came up out of the water. He roared, "Who's that trip-trapping on my bridge!?"

Big Goat answered in a boomy voice, "It is I, Big Goat!" The troll shouted, "Get off my bridge or I will eat you!" Goat answered, "This bridge is not yours. It belongs to everyone. Let me pass or I will bump you. Big Goat put his head down. But before he could move, the troll disappeared into the river. From that day on, anyone could cross the bridge.

Determine the number and types of roles

For this story we opted to use two narrators, three readers as the goats, and a group of sound-makers; the audience was assigned the troll role. The narrators have the hardest parts. The goats' lines are less demanding because of familiarity and repetition. The sound-makers have the easiest part, but note that, once again, it is calls for dynamic reading. This version contains a twist to the plot. We have attempted to heighten the impact of this adjusted message by giving the role of the troll to the largest number of readers, the audience.

Rearrange the text

After deleting unnecessary words, breaking the lines, and numbering them, we assigned role names. Through editing and piloting we developed this final format.
(See the complete reproducible script in Chapter 12.)

Three Billy Goats Gruff

7 Readers: READER 1,2; LITTLE GOAT, MIDDLE GOAT, BIG GOAT, SOUND-MAKERS, TROLL (as the AUDIENCE)

READER 1: The Three Billy Goats Gruff.
READER 2: Once upon a time,
READER 1: there were three billy goats.
LITTLE GOAT: I am Little Goat.
MIDDLE GOAT: I am Middle Goat.
BIG GOAT: I am Big Goat.
MIDDLE GOAT: We had eaten all the grass in the field,
…
READER 1: But he let Little Goat pass over the bridge.
SOUND-MAKERS: Trip, trap, trip, trap, trip, trap.
READER 1: Next Middle Goat started across the bridge.

SOUND-MAKERS: **Trip, trap, trip, trap, trip, trap.**
READER 2: Suddenly the troll came up out of the water.
TROLL: Who's that trip-trapping on my bridge!?
MIDDLE GOAT: It is I, Middle Goat.
TROLL: Get off my bridge or I will eat you!
LITTLE GOAT: Oh, please do not eat me. My bigger brother is coming. You will like him better.
READER 2: The troll growled.
…

Big Goat: Let me pass or I will bump you back in the water.
Middle Goat: And his horns are meaner than your growl!"
READER 2: Big Goat put his head down.
READER 1: But before he could move,
READER 2: the troll disappeared into the river.
READERS 1 & 2: From that day on, anyone could cross the bridge.
SOUND-MAKERS: **TRIP, TRAP, TRIP, TRAP, TRIP, TRAP.**

A FINAL WORD

There is no one way to write a RT. As with any art form the script can take on many forms and structures. Differences will depend on what the writer envisions as the final product for presentation. As the writer, you will take into account the needs and interests of the readers and audience. In our view, the RT experience should focus on students' learning the content and honing their ability to read. A major consideration is the age level of the students. What is suitable for one age group may not be appropriate for another. However we found that a RT script written specifically for lower elementary had application for middle and high school. These students enjoyed reading simple and familiar scripts.

Throughout this book you will find a variety of ways in which the scripts have been written. Ultimately the best script is the one that works for you as the instructor and for your students as learners. While we may give suggestions for ways in which they can be used effectively in the classroom, it is up to you, the professional, to determine just what form each script should take to maximize learning for your students.

III

Readers Theatre Preparation and Presentation

5

Writing Readers Theatre Scripts "from Scratch"

This chapter will give examples of scripts written from scratch and make connections with content.

Sometimes the teacher has an idea that actually emerges as a Readers Theatre (RT) script from the beginning. Once you have used this format, content that could otherwise be rather dry seems to come alive, as concepts tumble into meaningful lines. In some ways, this is the easiest process. There is no need to copy, divide lines, or reword original text—because it evolves in this style. And you don't need to worry about altering the author's intent—because you ARE the author.

EXAMPLE 1—THERE'S ONLY ONE 'I'

Content and Facts

During a unit on responsibility the following script, "There's Only One 'I,'" was prepared for third graders, The various aspects of responsibility for Community, City, Nation, and the Universe were to be a part of the learning.

Number of Readers and Style

Entire class involvement was one goal of this activity. The script was therefore designed so every student in the class would have lines to read.

Staging

Students holding the letter cards to form "ALL CREATION" stand in the back row. Those holding word cards sit in the front.

Possible extensions

Having the children raise cards at appropriate moments increases the interest in the reading. Dressing all the children in white shirts and red ties helps the audience focus on the readers. Setting the script to music enhances the spoken words.

Implementation

Make cards with the following words/letters: NATION, UNIVERSE, COMMUNITY, CITY, THE UNITED STATES, A, L, L, C, R, E, A, T, I, O, N.
Wherever an "I" appears it is printed in red; all other letters are black.
If there are more than 16 students, two or three students may hold a given word card and share the matching line(s).
(See the complete reproducible script in Chapter 12.)

There's Only One 'I'
16 Readers

VOICES 1-11: There's only one "I" in all creation.
VOICE 12: There's only one "I" in our nation.
VOICE 13: There's only one "I" in our whole universe.
VOICES 1-11: There's only one "I" in all creation.

VOICE 14: There's only one "I" in our community.
VOICE 15: There's only one "I" in our great city.
VOICE 16: There's only one "I" in the United States.
VOICES 1-11: There's only one "I" in all creation.

VOICES 1-11: There's only one "I" in all creation.
VOICE 12: There's only one "I" in our nation.

VOICE 13: There's only one "I" in our whole universe.
VOICES 1-11: There's only one "I" in all creation.
ALL: I must be responsible!

EXAMPLE 2—COLUMBUS' PRESS CONFERENCE

Concepts and Facts

Initially, we listed some facts essential to the students' learning: country of Columbus' origin, sponsors of the voyage and their nationality, year of the travel, and names of the ships.

Number of Readers and Style of Scripts

We decided to hold a news conference with Columbus conducted by three reporters from the Madrid Inquirer. Through this interview we interjected the facts and humor. By combining current news conference reporting style with the first journey of Columbus we came up this script.

Implementation

The script gives each of the four readers about 30 lines to read. The length of the script did not seem to deter the interest of the students, neither those reading nor those listening.
(See the complete reproducible script in Chapter 12.)

Columbus' Press Conference

4 Readers: REPORTER 1,2,3, COLUMBUS

REPORTER 1: Christopher Columbus is slated to have a news conference this morning.
REPORTER 2: We are aboard his ship Santa Maria
REPORTER 3: getting ready for his trip into the unknown sea.
REPORTER 2: While we are waiting for Admiral Columbus a little background is in order.
REPORTER 3: The year is 1492.
REPORTER 1: Most know that Columbus jumped ship,
REPORTER 3: pardon the pun,

...

COLUMBUS: and you and our ship will never be forgotten

REPORTER 2: Sir, Sir.

COLUMBUS: because we set forth with courage and faith to discover the New World.

ALL REPORTERS: Admiral Christopher Columbus!

COLUMBUS: Oh, pardon me, young men.

REPORTER 1: Could we have a word with you?

COLUMBUS: I didn't know you were around.

ALL REPORTERS: We are from the Madrid Inquirer.

COLUMBUS: Why didn't you speak up so I knew you were around?

REPORTER 1: Well, we...

COLUMBUS: Speak up. I will answer any questions.

REPORTER 2: You have been giving an enthusiastic challenge

REPORTER 3: to your sailors on this long trip.

REPORTER 1: How long have you been out to sea?

COLUMBUS: Fifteen minutes.

ALL REPORTERS: Fifteen minutes!

REPORTER 3: How do you handle being away from home out on the ocean

...

COLUMBUS: Oh, just a simple little poem about me.

REPORTER 2: Of course. Who else!?

COLUMBUS: A poem all school kids could memorize, to remember my name.

REPORTER 1: Can you quote some of the lines?

COLUMBUS: I've been doing some writing.

REPORTER 1: We're listening.

COLUMBUS: In fourteen hundred and eighty-three, Columbus sailed as fast as a bee.

REPORTER 3: That's it?

COLUMBUS: It's a start. Do you have other suggestions?

REPORTER 1: Well—

COLUMBUS: It's got to have a ring to it.

...

REPORTER 3: the year 1492 is nine years from now.

COLUMBUS: Who cares! All I want is a poem. Okay, men, we're turning around!

REPORTER 3: Go back toward Spain?

COLUMBUS: We'll come back in nine years!

REPORTER 2: Some story! Headlines…
REPORTER 3: In fourteen hundred and ninety-two,
REPORTER 1: Columbus will sail the ocean blue.
COLUMBUS: I just love press conferences.

EXAMPLE 3—MY FIRST FRIEND

Concepts and Facts

For a unit on friendship, the teacher listed words, phrases, and sentences about emotions and physical responses to them. These words and terms were then arranged to help describe the development of a friendship. We have found that listing the key words you want to get across to the students is a good starting place for writing a RT script. Focus on what you want the students to learn, add some humor, sprinkle in a little movement, and you have a recipe for learning.

Number of Readers and Style of Scripts

It was decided to have three readers perform lines assigned in random fashion. The style of the script would be simple presentational with emphasis on the use of various voice inflections.

Implementation

The script gives the three readers a wide range of emotional words to interpret and then connects them to the universal experience of making a new personal friend. A writing class could easily obtain ideas from hearing a presentation of this RT.
(See the complete reproducible script in Chapter 9.)

My First Friend
by Chip Gifford
3 readers

READER 1: Excitement
READER 2: Fear
READER 3: Tension

READER 1: Stress
READER 3: Anticipation
READER 2: Anxiety
READER 1: Nerves
READER 2: Sweaty palms
READER 3: Dry mouth

…

READER 1: Who can I sit with at lunch today?
READER 2: Scanning the tables
READER 3: Craning for a glimpse
READER 1: Scouring dozens of faces
READER 2: Fighting the urge
READER 1: To run
READER 3: To run and never look back
READER 2: But then
READER 1: Eye contact
READER 2: An inquisitive sparkle
READER 3: (hard swallow, gulp sound effect)
READER 2: A grin,
READER 3: Breaks
READER 1: Into a smile
READER 2: A hand

…

READER 3: I knew…
READER 1: Within
READER 2: The silence
READER 1: Within
READER 3: This stranger
READER 1: Within
READER 3: This quiet
READER 2: Unspoken communication
READER 1: I had found—
ALL: My first friend

A FINAL WORD

Creating your own script "from scratch" may seem time-consuming, but in many instances may save time. You do not need to search for just the right piece or make adjustments. You simply design it to suit your needs, choosing the vocabulary words and concepts to be taught, creating lines with your students in mind, providing as many movements or props as are appropriate for your situation, and sprinkling the script with the personality and humor of your class.

6

Guiding Students to Generate
Readers Theatre Scripts

After students have performed several Readers Theatre (RT) scripts they can develop literacy and content by generating their own scripts from a wide variety of literature. This chapter will give examples of five ways in which students can learn to generate their own RT scripts:

- Rearranging text

- Cutting up a book

- Completing sentences and adding lines

- Answering questions

- Adapting text

- Writing an interpretation of a non-fiction text

REARRANGING TEXT

Poetry is probably the easiest starting point for teaching students to prepare texts for Readers Theatre presentations. In general, we do not alter or add to the poet's words. Thus the only tasks are dividing and assignment of lines, deciding about pace and dynamics, and perhaps adding special effects.

The poem, "Winter," leads students to think about the change of seasons from the viewpoint of animals. It also provides opportunity for them to consider the mood of the setting. This blending of science content and a language arts skill seemed totally natural to the second graders who prepared the following interpretation. During this lesson, the children saw nothing unusual about the teacher's interspersing science-related terms like "habitat" and "protection" with literacy words like "place" and "feelings." Their preparation and performance of this piece were dynamic indications that they understood contrast—from both scientific and literary perspectives. Voicing and staging notes are included in the RT script developed from this poem by an anonymous author:

Winter

A white blanket of snow
is covering the ground
as animals snuggle in their winter homes
waiting for springtime
when sleepy, lazy days come to an end
and life returns to the forest.

Winter

3 Groups of Readers

GROUP 1: *Softly, without feeling.*
A white blanket of snow

GROUP 2: *Softly.*
is covering the ground
Slight pause.

GROUP 3: *Quietly, warmly.*
as animals snuggle

GROUP 2: *Quietly, warmly.*
in their winter homes
Slight pause.

GROUP 1: *Slower, quietly.*
waiting for springtime
Slight pause.

GROUP 3: *Even slower and quieter.*
when sleepy, lazy days

GROUP 2: *Louder and much faster.*
come to an end

All: *Joyously.*
and life returns to the forest.

CUTTING UP A BOOK

Another way to get students, particularly young students, involved in the process of preparing a Readers Theatre is to duplicate the text of a poem, short story, or picture book. The children then cut up the text and paste the lines on ruled paper. They make the assignments by writing the name(s) of the reader(s) before each line to be read. Having participated in the preparation of the script, they are ready and eager to perform it!

COMPLETING SENTENCES AND ADDING LINES

To help students learn to write the RT you can ask them to complete a script by adding appropriate words that interpret the original lines. The short nursery rhyme, "There was an Old Woman," is a good example. Students are asked to write their interpretations on the blank lines.

There Was An Old Woman
4 Readers

READER 1: There was an Old Woman
READER 3: _____
READER 2: There was an Old Woman
READER 4: _____
READER 3: Lived under a hill,
READER 1: _____

READER 4: And if she's not gone
READER 1: _____
READER 2: She lives there still.

Here is one example of one class' final product.

READER 1: There was an Old Woman
READER 3: whose husband was no more!
READER 2: There was an Old Woman
READER 4: a very good woman.
READER 3: Lived under a hill,
READER 1: where each day she took a pill.
READER 4: And if she's not gone
READER 1: where is she to go?
READER 2: She lives there still.
READER 3: That is just over the hill.

When this completed RT was read, those presenting the interpretational lines intuitively assumed the tone used by actors give "asides" to the audience. What a clever way to help children discover the difficult skill of making inferences!

ANSWERING QUESTIONS

Students can also prepare expository RT scripts using cloze procedures after answering key research questions. The teacher provides a frame on a current topic of study for students to complete. Here is an example of a frame students used to share information about storms.

> I appear when [*physical cause*].
> I make [*physical effect*].
> All around me [*effect on humans*].
> I am [*type of storm*].

The students were put into cooperative groups for this no-fail experience. Each group was asked to:

- research a specific type of storm,
- complete the frame,

- plan the presentation (i.e., divide and assign lines), and

- perform.

Here is one group's product.

Voice 1: I appear when very, very cold winds blow.
Voice 2: I make icicles form
Voice 1: and snow drifts pile high.
Voice 3: All around me cars are stuck,
Voice 1: people are stranded,
Voice 2: and a small bird freezes to death.
All Voices: I am blizzard.

This group simply read their script—but with great expression! Another team chose to wear yellow shirts and zigzag in front of a black bulletin board as they read their lines to "Thunderstorm." All performances were short, eliminating any potential for competition or boredom. At the same time, the information was shared in a vibrant and memorable manner. In fact, students asked for copies of their peers' scripts. These requests were unsolicited by the teacher, and the spontaneous suggestion was a source of pride for everyone. Any topic can be prepared in this fashion. Here are two other frames we have used successfully.

On the topic of animals—

When I am full-grown I *(physical appearance)*.
I stay alive by *(means of survival)*.
When people see men they *(relationship to humans)*.
I am *(kind of animal)*.

On the topic of countries.

Our land is led by *(top government official)*.
Our laws are made by *(legislative body)*.
We are people who *(source of economy, clothing, tradition)*.
We are famous for *(place, product, unique feature, event)*.
We are *(name of country)*.

Variation

Use in riddle format by asking the class to be ready to complete the last line chorally.

ADAPTING TEXT

Students can learn to adapt narrative texts as RT scripts by follow a process similar to the one suggested for teachers in Chapter 3. Usually this is a full-class activity. Occasionally, an individual student or small group will catch the fire and use this format when given a choice of writing form, but it is probably unwise to <u>require</u> that all students learn to adapt texts for RT independently. Here are steps we have used to lead students through the process of adapting a story for a simple presentation.

1. Choose a story with:

    • clearly identifiable characters or groups of characters,

    • dialogue, and

    • a series of actions that flow in an easy-to-follow sequence.

2. Prepare double-spaced copies of the original text. Enlarge one copy and make overhead transparencies.

3. Distribute hard copies. It seems to help keep students on task if they are marking their own copies as the class makes decisions.

4. Ask the students to read through the entire story—or read it aloud while students follow the text.

5. On the board or a chart list all of the characters in the story.

6. Decide whether individuals or groups should read characters' lines.

7. Decide how many narrators to use. Decide whether you want to include any full group lines. (Remember that every student should have at least one line to read.)

8. Adjust the text on an overhead by

    • deleting lengthy descriptive portions or reducing them to stage directions,

- deleting lead-ins/tags to dialogue, e.g., "she/he said,"

- breaking long sentences into shorter lines no more than10 words, and

- making the choral reading easier by repeating important phrases. (The "safest" option is to have a soloist say the phrase once, to set the rhythm, and have a group echo it.)

9. Identify the reader label for each line.

10. Make new copies.

11. Assign roles.

12. Perform.

This is a time-consuming activity. To ensure that every minute has academic value, be sure that the selection is directly tied to the curriculum. To add transcurricular impact intersperse instruction on language elements, e.g., the function of quotation marks, the use of adjectives in stage directions, and the need for expressive, fluent reading to enhance comprehension.

Following is the text of a myth used in a fourth-grade classroom. At the time, the curriculum included emphases on reasons for colors in nature (science), attributes of myths (literature), and correct use of punctuation marks (language arts). Note how aptly this selection lends itself to all three subject areas.

WHY OCEANS ARE BLUE—THE TEXT
A Myth

Did you know that long ago, when the earth was young, the four oceans were not blue, but crystal clear? The brilliantly colored underwater plants and fish could easily be seen from above. People marveled at the beautiful sight; however, all was not well. Life was too easy for the fishermen. The vibrant fish had no place to hide from the fishermen in the transparent seas. The population of fishermen increased while the helpless fish were quickly becoming endangered. As time passed, many of the oceans' beautiful inhabitants became extinct. Each ocean decided to send a representative to the other elements to seek help with their problem. First, they went to the land. "Can you help us?" they pleaded. "Our waters are so clear that the fishermen have no competition. We must protect our fish? "If I share my soil with you," offered the land, the oceans will become brown and muddy.

Then your fish and plants will have difficulty seeing each other in the darkness. Is that what you want?" "Oh, no!" answered the oceans. "that would cause more problems." The mountains and the forest sadly could not help either. Finally the oceans consulted the faraway sky. The brilliant, sapphire-blue sky was not only beautiful, but also very wise. She listened to the oceans and, after some thought, she responded, "I have an idea, but I will ask something in return. You may use a part of my sapphire-blue color to turn your waters blue enough to keep your fish out of sight. In return, you must lend me some of the bright colors of your fish and plants." The oceans quickly agreed. From that day to this, the blue of the oceans has provided a home to many creatures. And colorful rainbows grace the still lovely sky.

Here is the way the class chose to convert the text to RT format.

Why Oceans Are Blue

Readers/Roles: NARRATORS 1-6, OCEANS 1-4, LAND 1-3, SKY-1,
MOUNTAINS-ANY NUMBER, FORESTS-ANY NUMBER

NARRATOR 1: Long ago, when the earth was young,
NARRATOR 2: the four oceans were not blue,
NARRATOR 3: but crystal clear.
NARRATOR 1: The brilliantly colored underwater plants
NARRATOR 2: and fish
NARRATOR 4: could easily be seen from above.
NARRATOR 2: People marveled at the beautiful sight;
NARRATOR 4: however, all was not well.
NARRATOR 3: The vibrant fish had no place to hide from the fishermen in the transparent seas.
NARRATOR 5: The population of fishermen increased
NARRATOR 4: while the helpless fish quickly became endangered.
NARRATOR 6: As time passed,
NARRATOR 4: many of the oceans' beautiful inhabitants became extinct.
NARRATOR 1: Then each ocean sent a representative
NARRATOR 6: to ask their friends for help.
OCEANS 1,2: Land, can you help us?
OCEAN 3: Our waters are so clear
OCEAN 4: that the fishermen can see our fish too easily.
OCEANS 1,2: Can you help us protect our fish?
LAND 1: If we share our soil with you,

LAND 2: the oceans will become brown and muddy.

LAND 3: Then the fish will have difficulty seeing each other or the plants.

LAND 4: Is that what you want?

OCEANS 3,4: Oh, no! That would cause more problems.

Pause.

OCEANS 1,2: Mountains, can you help us?

MOUNTAINS: Sorry. We can't help you.

Pause.

OCEANS 1,2: Forests, can you help us?

FORESTS: Sorry. We can't help you, either.

NARRATOR 6: Finally, the oceans consulted the faraway sky.

NARRATOR 2: The brilliant sapphire blue sky was not only beautiful,

NARRATOR 1: but also very wise.

OCEANS 1,2: Sky, can you help us?

OCEAN 4: Our waters are so clear

OCEAN 3: that the fishermen can see our fish too easily.

OCEANS 1,2: Can you help us protect our fish?

Pause.

SKY: Hmm. I have an idea, but I will ask something in return.

ALL OCEANS: What is your idea?

SKY: You may use a part of my sapphire-blue color to turn your waters blue enough to keep your fish out of sight.

ALL OCEANS: And in return?

SKY: In return, you must lend me some of the bright colors of your fish and plants.

ALL OCEANS: Oh, yes, yes, yes.

ALL NARRATORS: From that day to this, the blue of the oceans has provided a home to many creatures.

NARRATOR 1: And the still lovely sky is graced by colorful rainbows.

WRITING AN INTERPRETATION OF NON-FICTIONAL TEXT

Students can also convert non-fiction passages into RT, often without changing the original words. You can guide them by following these steps.

- Distribute copies, one per student, so students can mark as they go.

- Display a copy on the overhead screen.

- Guide the class to break the lines into short phrases.

- Decide on choral and solo lines (and perhaps audience lines).

- Choose lines that might warrant repetition.

- Count the number of roles and compare with the number of students in the group. Readjust to ensure that all have lines to read.

- Assign parts.

- Practice.

- Present.

Again as students help make the decisions about breaks, assignments, voicing etc., they become more invested in the process if they manipulate their own scripts.

"Weather Wonderings: A Grain of Truth" is an appropriate piece for modeling how to mark non-fiction scripts for RT. Simply dividing the lines at appropriate times and assigning roles give life to this selection. We asked students to read the following passage silently, thinking about how they would change the text into a RT presentation. Knowing students would likely find it a daunting task to change the entire text into a RT as one assignment, we divided it into three parts. This allowed for discussion of the content and opportunities to make improvements as each section unfolded.

Here is the way a fourth grade class adjusted the text as a RT. *(See the complete reproducible script in Chapter 10.)*

Weather Wonderings: A Grain of Truth Text—Part 1

If you have ever lived in a farm community, you know that there are silly little sayings about ways you can tell when the weather will change. But are they just wives' tales—or do they contain a grain of truth?

When sheep gather in huddles,
Tomorrow we'll have puddles.

Sheep's wool traps air as insulation, so when the air turns cold, sheep feel chilly. To keep warm, they move close together.

When clouds look like black smoke
A wise man puts on his cloak.

VOICE 1: If you have ever lived in a farm community,
VOICE 2: you know that there are silly little sayings
VOICE 3: about ways you can tell when the weather will
...
ALL: When sheep gather in huddles,
Tomorrow we'll have puddles.
VOICE 4: A sheep's wool traps air as insulation,
VOICE 5: so when the air turns cold,
VOICE 6: sheep feel chilly.
VOICE 4: To keep warm,
VOICES 4-6: they move close together.
ALL: When clouds look like black smoke a wise man puts on his cloak.

Weather Wonderings: A Grain of Truth Text—Part 2

Meteorologists know that several cloud patterns usually produce rain or snow. Flat, gray, altostratus clouds, which form in layers, may cause rain or snow. When altostratus clouds thicken and drift low, they form dark, ragged nimbostratus clouds from which continuous rain or snow falls. Cumulonimbus clouds may build into towering formations that bring thunderstorms.

When the cow scratches her ear,
It means a shower is near;
But when she thumps her ribs with her tail
Expect thunder, lightning and hail.

Low atmospheric pressure and increased humidity cause the hairs inside a cow's ear to wiggle. This may tickle and make her scratch. Before a violent storm, static charges may make a cow's hair stand straight up. To try to relieve the discomfort this causes, she may brush herself with her tail over and over again.

The owls hoot, the peacocks toot,
The ducks quack, frogs yak—
'Twill rain.
The loons call, swallows fall,

Chickens hover, groundhogs take cover—
'Twill rain.

VOICE 7: Meteorologists know that several cloud patterns usually produce
VOICES 7-9: rain or snow.
VOICE 8: Flat,
VOICE 9: gray,
VOICE 7: altostratus clouds,
VOICE 8: which form in layers,
VOICE 9: may cause
…
VOICE 10: This may tickle
VOICE 11: and make her scratch.
VOICE 12: Before a violent storm,
VOICE 10: static charges may make a cow's hair
…
VOICES 10-12: frogs yak—
ALL: 'twill rain.
VOICES 13-15: The loons call,
ALL READERS: swallows fall,
VOICES 19-21: chickens hover,
VOICES 22-24: groundhogs take cover—
ALL: 'twill rain

Weather Wonderings: A Grain of Truth Text—Part 3

Cows are not the only creatures that sense coming rain. Many animals respond to the low pressure and high humidity just before a storm. They become uncomfortable, restless, and noisy.

A circle around the moon—
'Twill rain soon.

The high, feathery clouds called cirrostratus clouds are made entirely of ice crystals. The ice crystals refract light and create haloes around the moon. These clouds do not directly cause precipitation, but they frequently become water-heavy at lower altitudes, and soon comes a storm.

Rainbow in the morning,
Shepherds take warning.

Rainbow at night
Shepherds' delight.

When rain clouds filled with moisture are in the west and the morning sun
shines on them from the east, a rainbow forms. The water droplets scatter
the sun's rays and the colors of the spectrum appear. Many storms move
west to east, so a morning rainbow in the east usually comes before a rain.
If the setting sun shines on clouds in the east, it means that the clouds have
already passed by and the rain is over. Are weather jingles just wives' tales,
or do they, in fact, contain a grain of truth?

VOICE 13: Cows are not the only creatures that sense coming rain.
VOICE 14: Many animals respond to the low pressure
VOICE 15: and high humidity
VOICES 13-15: just before a storm.
VOICE 13: They become uncomfortable,
VOICE 14: restless, and

…

VOICE 21: If the setting sun shines on clouds in the east,
VOICE 19: it means that the clouds have already passed by
VOICES 19-21: and the rain is over.

…

VOICE 22: Are weather jingles
VOICE 23: just wives' tales,
VOICE 24: or do they, in fact, contain
ALL: a grain of truth?

Option

If students have already had experience with converting prose into RT scripts,
this may be one of several weather passages to be prepared and shared by small
groups. Each of the three sections is of manageable size for a group of students
to prepare.

A FINAL WORD

There is nothing more validating to students than collaborating as a community of learners to design a worthy product and showcase it publicly. To ensure
this sense of ownership, it is the teacher's responsibility to see that every stu-

dent is asked to contribute to the writing process, is honored for his/her ideas, and is included in the performance.

7

Casting, Voicing, and Staging

The attractiveness of Readers Theatre (RT) as an instructional tool is its simplicity: no props, no costumes, only the voices of the readers. Its appeal is powerful for classroom teachers, who have limited time, limited resources, and limited means of motivating student learning. All three of these needs are addressed through RT presentations. Instructional time is devoted solely to decoding, interpreting text, and building fluency. There are genuine purposes for repeated readings; often, repetitive lines are built into the text, and, even more often, the students ask to "do it again." All necessary resources can be found within the regular classroom. The essential component is a good text; other materials are optional and may be symbolic rather than realistic. Personalized roles for performance are very motivational, because all are active participants.

Once students are familiar with the RT approach they may want to add special effects. Thus it is incumbent on the teacher to help them develop the ability to offer appropriate suggestions about casting, voicing and staging. When they become engaged in the process, students often choose to use their own time and resources to embellish the performance, reducing the demands on instructional time and increasing student pride in the final outcome.

This appeals to classroom teachers, whose instructional resources are minimal. It is our experience that two things happen when RTs are used as a part of the instruction. First, students want to go beyond only acting with the voice to include movement and costumes. Students at all ages have an irresistible urge to move and to don symbols of roles. Second, teachers always need to put together programs for parent nights or special holiday times for which they want showier performances than simple RT presentations.

These two factors lead us to a performance mode beyond just reading. Our definition of RT stresses interpretation of the literature. This is accomplished primarily through the use of the voice, but can also incorporate simple theatrical touches for casting, voicing, and staging. This chapter gives examples of special techniques for enhancing RT performances.

CASTING

Casting requires thoughtful consideration. The method for assignment of roles is dependent upon your purpose and population. Asking students to volunteer for specific roles is appropriate if the entire text is at the independent reading level for all participants, and if students have already developed skills for making cooperative decisions.

In general, however, the assignment of parts is completed more efficiently and effectively when the teacher assumes this responsibility. If the script is being prepared for public performance, the major criterion for selecting roles is the reader's ability to execute the lines with expression.

If the purpose for using RT is to help less proficient readers develop fluency and comprehension, roles for these students should include lines with some or all of these features:

- Repeated phrases.
- High-interest content.
- Familiar vocabulary.
- Limited number of words.

It is a good idea to assign some short, simple lines and chorally read passages to both proficient and less-experienced readers. When emerging readers see that strong readers are happily engaged in parts similar to their own, no stigma can be tied to these differentiated roles.

There is sometimes a temptation to typecast students when assigning parts, but we recommend avoiding this practice. Since RT is the art of using voice only to portray meaning, the student's appearance and personality are not factors; he must simply speak his lines convincingly.

When students are assisting with casting it is important to begin with a script which

- is relatively short,
- contains lines of approximately equal difficulty and lengths, and
- relies heavily on emotional interpretation.

If the selection is short, it is possible to break the class into groups, each preparing the same script; performances are then compared. If the lines are of similar difficulty, peer coaching is sufficient for less-proficient readers. If the focus is on meaning, the reader's gender, voice pitch, and personality are non-issues.

Patrick Henry's speech is an excellent example of such a script. Students eagerly listen to multiple readings, noting differences in interpretations. As students listen to others' performances of this script, the teacher can help them identify ways the readers have used their voices to show various emotions and attitudes: hardness, sarcasm, superiority, innocence, doubt, pride, defiance, irritability, joy, anger, etc. Thus she is preparing students to label voicing directions.

(See the complete reproducible script in Chapter 12.)

Liberty or Death

By Patrick Henry adapted for Readers Theatre
6 Readers: READER 1,2,3,4; HENRY 1,2

Prologue

READER 1: Patrick Henry, a leading Virginia lawyer,
READER 2: a fiery orator, a legislator,
READER 3: a staunch advocate of political liberty.
READER 4: He gave this speech before the Virginia Convention of 1776.
…

Address

HENRY 1: Mr. President, no man thinks more highly that I do of patriotism.
HENRY 2: But different men often see the same objects in different lights.
HENRY 1: I hope that it will not be thought disrespectful to those gentlemen,

HENRY 2: to entertain opinions of a character very opposite to theirs.
HENRY 1: I speak forth my sentiments freely and without reserve.
…
READER 2: Remonstrated.
READER 3: Supplicated.
READER 4: And prostrated ourselves before the tyrannical hands of the Parliament.
HENRY 1: Our petitions have been slighted.
HENRY 2: Our remonstrance's have produced violence and insult.
HENRY 1: Our supplications have been spurned.
…
READER 4: What is your wish?
READER 3: What would you have us do?
HENRY 1: I know not what course others may take,
HENRY 2: but as for me,
HENRY 1: Give me liberty,
HENRY 2: or give me death.
ALL READERS: Then give us liberty or death!

VOICING

Readers Theatre is acting with the voice. The voice is a marvelous conveyor of emotions and feelings and can be used in a variety of ways.

Types of Voicing

The following voicing techniques can be incorporated into scripts:

- unison—all readers reading at one time
- solo—one reader reading alone
- superimposed—two readers reading different words simultaneously
- echoing—repeating the exact words of a reader
- background—reading as a background affect to the main lines
- cumulative—a series of lines read with a progressive build-up of voices
- overlapped—lines read before the previous line is finished

- crescendoing—lines growing in volume through the addition of readers one at a time

Emotions To Be Heard In The Voice

The voice is a marvelous conveyor of emotions and feeling. It can change the mood in any of the following ways:

- loudness or force
- tonal variations
- pitch—highness and lowness of the voice
- pace of delivery
- varying stress on words or syllables
- projection of words
- clarity of sound

The voice can project many emotions such as:

• Defiance	Sullenness	Innocence
• Irritability	Shock	Sarcasm
• Doubt	Anger	Love
• Joy	Excitement	Superiority
• Pride	Humor	Hatred

Warm-up Exercise-1

Emotions and voicing can be taught through a warm-up exercise prior to performing a RT. Demonstrate to the students how the voice and body can communicate emotions and feelings. Then have students read the following, one line at a time. Continue reading until each student has an opportunity to read at least three different lines. This can be done with the entire class or in groups of 5 or 6.

Hal's head spoke harshness.

Sally was stupidly sullen.

Sam is simply sarcastic.

A saxophone sound is sexy.

His shoulders indicate superiority.

Quinton is always questioning.

Ivan the Terrible was not a person of innocence.

Gale and George were just plainly gossipy.

Dan was doubtful.

Paul was filled with pride.

Denny shows extreme defiance.

Irene was the height of irritability.

Aaron was the angry one.

Joy was known for her joy.

Harry was full of humor.

Agnes was all too agreeable.

Stuart was easily shocked.

Lana was in love.

Edgar and excitement went together.

Herb hated everyone.

Etc.

Warm-up Exercise-2

This warm-up exercise involves group responses in the voice of females and then of males. Decide on a name that is not represented in the room. The group then says the name in the voice indicated after you, or a class member, reads each line.

Female Group Response:

DRAMA DIRECTOR: Mother called her son's name *quietly*, _____
Drama Director: But he was asleep so she called a *little louder*, _____

DRAMA DIRECTOR: No answer. So she went upstairs and bent over and *through clenched teeth* spoke his name. _____
DRAMA DIRECTOR: He was up in flash but slowed down when he started to get his clothes on. So Mom *shouted* his name, _____
DRAMA DIRECTOR: When he did appear in the kitchen Mom put her arms around him and *tenderly* said his name, _____
DRAMA DIRECTOR: Then she *joyfully* repeated his name, _____
DRAMA DIRECTOR: But when she noticed that he had not done the dishes from the night before she spoke his name *sharply*, _____
DRAMA DIRECTOR: She wondered if he had brushed his teeth so she *questioningly* called his name, _____
DRAMA DIRECTOR: When he said he hadn't brushed his teeth for 3 days, she spoke his name *disgustedly*, _____
DRAMA DIRECTOR: He immediately started to brush his teeth and do the dishes at the same time. Of course, mothers being mothers, she still loved him and you could hear it as she said his name *lovingly*, _____
DRAMA DIRECTOR: Well, everyone was happy, happy, happy, and when he got to school his English teacher *flatly spoke his name*, _____

Male group response:

DRAMA DIRECTOR: Father called his daughter's name *quietly*, _____
DRAMA DIRECTOR: But she was asleep so he called a *little louder*, _____

DRAMA DIRECTOR: No answer. So he went upstairs and bent over and *through clenched teeth* spoke her name, _____

DRAMA DIRECTOR: She was up in flash but slowed down when she started to get her clothes on. So Dad *shouted* her name, _____

DRAMA DIRECTOR: When she did appear in the kitchen Dad put his arms around her and *tenderly* said, _____

DRAMA DIRECTOR: Then he *joyfully* repeated her name, _____

DRAMA DIRECTOR: But when he noticed that she had not done the dishes from the night before he spoke her name *sharply*, _____

DRAMA DIRECTOR: He wondered if he had brushed her teeth so he *questioningly* called her name, _____

DRAMA DIRECTOR: When she said she hadn't brushed her teeth for 3 days, he spoke her name *disgustedly*, _____

DRAMA DIRECTOR: She immediately started to brush her teeth and do the dishes at the same time. Of course, fathers being fathers, he still loved her and you could hear it as he said her name *lovingly*, _____

DRAMA DIRECTOR: Well, everyone was happy, happy, happy, and when she got to school her English teacher *flatly* said her name, _____

Warm-up Exercise-3

The following exercise can also be used as a warm-up for the voice. Lines may be read chorally, or students may take turns reading them as solo lines. A teacher may choose to combine modeling and full-class involvement by randomly selecting lines to read, accompanying them with body movements; the students then echo the words and copy the movements. Students may volunteer to take the leader role or to add lines. Notice how this exercise accentuates the literary technique of alliteration.

> Agreeable Agnes.
> Angry Aaron.
> Defiant Denny.
> Doubting Dan.
> Eager Edgar.
> Gossipy George.
> Harsh Harriet.
> Hateful Herb.
> Humorous Harry.

Innocent Ivan.

Irritating Irene.

Joyful Joy.

Lovely Lana.

Proud Paul.

Questioning Quentin.

Sarcastic Sam.

Sexy Suzy.

Shocked Stuart.

Sullen Sally.

Superior Stan.

STAGING

Staging should be added only when it enhances presentation of the literature. It should reinforce rather than detract from the theme. Knowledge of "stage language" will help you and your students visualize enhancements to the performances. You should be familiar with basic terms and staging techniques.

Basic Terms

Following are basic theatrical terms with which the teacher and participants should have a working knowledge:

- Stage movement: Any change of position or location on the stage

- Dominant position: A position of prominence on stage—usually the spot on the stage where the reader can best be seen by the audience

- Subordinate position: A weaker position of one reader to another on stage

- Full front position: When the reader is facing the audience

- One-quarter position: When the reader has turned one-fourth of a turn from the audience

- Half-turn position: When the reader has turned one-half of a turn from the audience

- Three-quarters position: When the reader has turned three-quarters of a turn from the audience

- Full back position: When the reader is standing with his/her back to the audience

- Off stage focus: When the reader directs his/her voice toward the audience

- Positioning: Places the readers take when on stage or in front of a classroom

- From the top: An expression telling readers to start at the beginning of the script

Staging Technique

The diagram shows how the stage is divided into nine sections to assist with positioning students for a performance.

Up Stage Right (USR)	Up Stage Center (USC)	Up Stage Left (USL)
Center Stage Right (CSR)	Center Stage (CSC)	Center Stage Left (CSL)
Down Stage Right (DSR)	Down Stage Center (DSC)	Down Stage Left (DSL)

(front of the stage)

Staging should provide the best setting to maximize interpretation of the reading, and may involve the following elements:

- Levels—Readers are placed on boxes, ladders, chairs etc. at different heights to emphasize various part of the reading.

- Stands/Lecterns—This is used to hold the script so the reader has the entire body available for gestures to help interpret the literature.

- Scripts as props—Scripts can be used as props in a variety of ways: For example, moving the scripts away from the body as a line is read reinforces the point; and dropping the script can show exasperation.

- Script folders—Providing look-alike folders to hold the scripts adds professionalism to the performance.

- Focus—Where the participants look as they read can give special meanings.

- Positioning—The placement of the participants on the stage focuses the audience's attention. (See diagram above). For example, the principal readers are usually placed at Center Stage and the lesser figures farther back.

- Sound effects—Sounds can emphasize words or lines being read. They set a climate to enhance the interpretation: For example, snapping fingers can heighten the urgency of the lines being read; and humming can produce a meditative mood.

DIRECTOR'S INFORMATION

An example of staging, voicing, and to a lesser extent casting is illustrated for three RT scripts: The Three Wishes, The House That Jack Built, and The Gettysburg Address. Complete Director's Information pages are given for each RT. In the Director's Information pages the following types of cues will be found:

- Entering
- Positioning
- Focus
- Levels
- Scripts as props
- Sound effects
- Props
- Exiting
- Staging notes (in italicized, bold-faced type)

The director information instructions may or may not be written on the performers' script.

Director's Information

The Three Wishes—An English Folktale
8 Readers: 4 NARRATORS, ELF, WOODSMAN, WIFE, DOG
(See chapter 9 for a copy of the performers' script.)

Entering: Director's discretion.
Positioning: Initially the Narrators (N1-4) face Quarter Left, Woodsman (Wo) and Elf (El) full front, Wife (Wi) and Dog (Do) full back. Arrow indicates direction that the Woodsman and Elf take as directed in the script.

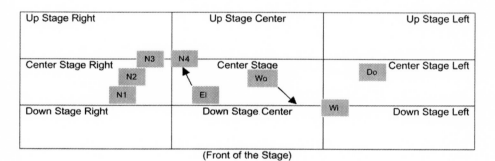

(Front of the Stage)

Focus: Narrators look over the audience as they read; all others are full front and read over the audience.
Levels: Narrators stand on chairs.
Props: A broom handle carried by the Woodsman.
Scripts as Props: As seems natural to the readers.
Sound effects: Built into the script lines.
Stands/lecterns: None.
Voicing: See bold-faced type in the script.

The Three Wishes—An English Folktale

8 Readers: NARRATORS 1-4, ELF, WOODSMAN, WIFE, DOG

NARRATOR 1: Once upon a time
NARRATOR 2: There was a Woodsman
Woodsman puts broom handle on his shoulder.
NARRATOR 3: who went out to cut down a tree.
NARRATOR 1: He found a mighty oak and raised his ax.

NARRATOR 4: Suddenly a wee voice called out…

ELF: Stop! Do not cut this tree.

Woodsman lifts broom handle from shoulder and rests it on the floor.

NARRATOR 2: The Woodsman dropped his ax and…

All NARRATORs: Poof!

NARRATOR 3: Immediately, there stood before him a tiny ELF.

NARRATOR 4: The little fellow begged…

ELF: This tree is my home.

WOODSMAN: Your home?

ELF: Yes, my home. Please do not cut it down.

WOODSMAN: *Puts the broom handle back on his shoulder.*

But I am a Woodsman.

ELF: If you leave my tree alone then…

WOODSMAN: Then what?

ELF: *Holds up three fingers.*

Then I will grant you three wishes.

WOODSMAN: Any three wishes at all?

ELF: Any three wishes at all.

WOODSMAN: All right, but may I have time to think about my wishes?

ELF: Take your time. Just think of a wish and it will come true.

WOODSMAN: *Turns quarter left as though to leave.*

Thank you!

ELF: But remember.

WOODSMAN: *Turns back to original position.*

What?

ELF: *Assumes full back position and takes one step quarter right.*

You have only three wishes. Use them wisely.

Woodsman takes one step quarter left toward Wife and Dog.

NARRATOR 1: The Woodsman started home

NARRATOR 4: without any wood,

NARRATOR 3: but with great excitement.

NARRATOR 2: He could not wait to tell his Wife the good news.

NARRATOR 4: They could make such wonderful plans.

NARRATOR 1: He thought to himself,

WOODSMAN: I wish I were home right now!

All NARRATORs: Poof!

NARRATOR 3: Immediately, he was at home,

Wife and Dog face full front.

NARRATOR 2: sitting by the fire with his Wife.
WOODSMAN: *Lays the handle down.*
Oh, no!
NARRATOR 1: he cried.
NARRATOR 4: His Wife,
NARRATOR 3: looking startled,
NARRATOR 4: asked...
WIFE: What is the matter, dear?
NARRATOR 1: When the Woodsman told her what had happened,
NARRATOR 3: she said...
WIFE: It is all right, dear. I am glad you are home.
WOODSMAN: Yes, I am home.
WIFE: *Holds up two fingers.*
And you still have two wishes.
WOODSMAN: Yes, I do.
WIFE: You will just need to be more careful what you think.
WOODSMAN: Yes, I will.
NARRATOR 3: The Woodsman sat by the fire
NARRATOR 1: while his Wife began to make supper.
NARRATOR 2: He could smell his favorite sausage cooking in the kitchen.
NARRATOR 4: The fire was warm
Woodsman yawns.
NARRATOR 3: and he began to feel sleepy.
NARRATOR 2: So comfortable was he that didn't want to move.
Woodsman puts hand to mouth.
NARRATOR 1: He put his hand to his face
NARRATOR 2: to cover a contented yawn.
NARRATOR 3: He thought to himself...
WOODSMAN: I wish I had that sausage right here.
ALL NARRATORS: Poof!
NARRATOR 3: Immediately, a sausage flew
NARRATOR 2: right onto the Woodsman's
All NARRATORS: NOSE!
WOODSMAN: Oh, no!
NARRATOR 1: he cried.
NARRATOR 4: His Wife,
NARRATOR 3: looking startled,
NARRATOR 4: asked...

WIFE: What is the matter, dear?
NARRATOR 1: When the Woodsman told her what had happened,
NARRATOR 2: she said…
WIFE: It is all right, dear. I will pull the sausage from your nose.
NARRATOR 4: She pulled
NARRATOR 3: and he pulled.
NARRATOR 1: He pulled
NARRATOR 2: and she pulled.
NARRATOR 3: Even the dog came
NARRATOR 1: and pulled
NARRATOR 4: and they all pulled.
DOG: Woof!
NARRATOR 2: But the sausage would not leave the man's nose.
NARRATOR 1: Finally the Woodsman nodded sadly,
NARRATOR 3: and the Wife nodded sadly.
NARRATOR 4: Even the dog nodded sadly.
DOG: Woof, woof, woof!
NARRATOR 2: They all knew what he had to do.
NARRATOR 1: The Woodsman said aloud…
WOODSMAN: I wish this sausage were off my nose!
All NARRATORs: Poof!
NARRATOR 3: Immediately,
NARRATOR 1: the sausage fell from his nose.
NARRATOR 4: As they ate dinner,
NARRATOR 2: the Woodsman said…
WOODSMAN: I have never tasted better sausage.
WIFE: Thank you.
WOODSMAN: I wish I had never wanted more than the happiness I have had all along.
NARRATOR 3: The Woodsman nodded knowingly.
NARRATOR 2: His Wife nodded knowingly.
NARRATOR 4: Even the dog nodded knowingly.
Narrators step down from chairs and face full front. Elf faces full front.
DOG: Woof! Woof!
ALL READERS: The End.
All bow to the audience and exit.

Director's Information

The House That Jack Built
4 Readers
(See Chapter 9 for a copy of the performers' script.)

The following script of "The House that Jack Built" includes voicing and staging notes. If the performance is to run smoothly and efficiently, the readers must practice both the words and the movements. Keep in mind that, while the author or teacher may have his vision of the delivery, it is often wise to give the performers some latitude in choosing how to interpret the reading. If the students have prepared the stage directions, they will want to include them on the scripts. Otherwise they are not typically written on the distributed copies, but are available only to the director. Notice the predictability and cadence in this rendition that make it a delightful poem for presenters and audience alike.

Entrance/Positioning: Readers enter either from DSL or DSR in the following order: READERS: R4, R3, R2, R1. All Readers face full front and are positioned as suggested in the diagram below.

Up Stage Right	Up Stage Center	Up Stage Left
Center Stage Right	Center Stage R1 R1 R3 R4	Center Stage Left
Down Stage Right	Down Stage Center	Down Stage Left Imaginary House

(Front of the Stage)

Focus: Off stage.
Levels: All on same level.
Props: None.
Scripts as Props: As seems natural to the readers.
Sound effects: None.
Stands/lecterns: None.
Voicing: See bold-faced type in the script.

Exit: After the presentation, the readers take a slight bow and leave the stage DSL in the following order: R1, R4, R2, R3.

The House That Jack Built
4 Readers

ALL READERS: *Point DSL to imaginary house.*
This is the house that Jack built.
READER 4: This is the malt,
ALL READERS: that lay in the house that Jack built.
READER 4: This is the rat,
READER 3: that ate the malt,
ALL READERS: *Point DSL left to imaginary house.*
that lay in the house that Jack built.
READER 4: This is the cat,
READER 2: *Terrible look on the face.*
that killed the rat,
READER 3: that ate the malt,
ALL READERS: *Point DSL left to imaginary house.*
that lay in the house that Jack built.
READER 4: This is the dog,
Next four lines read very rapidly.
READER 1: that worried the cat,
READER 2: *Terrible look on the face.*
that killed the rat,
READER 3: that ate the malt,
ALL READERS: *Point DSL left to imaginary house.*
that lay in the house that Jack built.
READER 3: This is the cow with the crumpled horn,
READER 4: that tossed the dog,
Next four lines read very rapidly.
READER 1: that worried the cat,
Terrible look on the face.
READER 2: that killed the rat,
READER 3: that ate the malt,
ALL READERS: *Point DSL left to imaginary house.*
that lay in the house that Jack built.

READER 2: This is the maiden all forlorn,
READER 3: that milked the cow with the crumpled horn,
READER 4: that tossed the dog,
Next four lines read very rapidly.
READER 1: that worried the cat,
READER 2: *Terrible look on the face.*
that killed the rat,
READER 3: that ate the malt,
ALL READERS: *Point DSL left to imaginary house.*
that lay in the house that Jack built.
READER 4: This is the man all tattered and torn,
READER 1: *Pucker up the lips.*
that kissed the maiden all forlorn,
READER 2: that milked the cow with the crumpled horn,
READER 4: that tossed the dog,
READER 1: *Terrible look on the face.*
that worried the cat,
READER 2: that killed the rat,
READER 3: that ate the malt,
ALL READERS: *Point DSL left to imaginary house.*
that lay in the house that Jack built.
READER 4: This is the priest all shaven and shorn,
READER 3: that married the man all tattered and torn,
READER 1: that kissed the maiden all forlorn,
READER 2: that milked the cow with the crumpled horn,
READER 4: that tossed the dog,
Next four lines read very rapidly.
READER 1: that worried the cat,
READER 2: *Terrible look on the face.*
that killed the rat,
READER 3: that ate the malt,
ALL READERS: *Point DSL left to imaginary house.*
that lay in the house that Jack built.
READER 4: This is the cock that crowed in the morn,
ALL READERS: Cock-doodle-do
READER 3: that waked the priest all shaven and shorn,
READER 4: that married the man all tattered and torn,
READER 1: *Pucker up the lips.*

that kissed the maiden all forlorn,
READER 2: that milked the cow with the crumpled horn,
READER 4: that tossed the dog,
Pause.
that tossed the dog,
Next four lines read very rapidly.
READER 1: that worried the cat,
READER 2: *Terrible look on the face.*
that killed the rat,
READER 3: that ate the malt,
ALL READERS: *Point DSL left to imaginary house.*
that lay in the house that Jack built.
READER 4: This is the farmer sowing,
READER 2: that kept the cock that crowed in the morn,
ALL READERS: Cock-doodle-do.
READER 3: that waked the priest all shaven and shorn,
READER 4: that married the man all tattered and torn,
READER 1: *Pucker up the lips.*
that kissed the maiden all forlorn,
READER 2: that milked the cow with the crumpled horn,
READER 4: that tossed the dog,
Pause.
that tossed the dog,
Pause and then very loud.
that tossed the dog,
Next four lines read very rapidly.
READER 1: that worried the cat,
READER 2: *Terrible look on the face.*
that killed the rat,
READER 3: that ate the malt,
ALL READERS: *Point DSL left to imaginary house.*
that lay in the house that Jack built.
READER 4: Did Jack really build that house?
READER 2: No, I think it was actually Jill that built the house.
ALL READERS: The End.

Implementation

This particular reading was used in a literature class to illustrate the functions of various parts of speech, but also in a science class to initiate discussion of the food chains. The latter use may seem strange but don't overlook the powerful use of dramatic presentations of familiar reading materials to create interest in content-area topics. The use of this script in a science class was effective in hooking the students' interest in naturally occurring facts of how life is sustained.

PRESENTATIONAL TO REPRESENTATIONAL—STAGING TO ENHANCE INTERPRETATION

For simple use in the classroom, staging is generally not needed; but for some scripts, positioning and gestures make the presentation livelier and more understandable for the audience. The teacher needs to sense the students' level of involvement. Often they want to move beyond simply reading to acting. Allowing them to enhance the interpretation through entrances, positioning, movements, exits, small props, and simple costumes increases their ownership of the performance. This extra effort may be worthwhile use of time, if the class is preparing a performance for another class, an assembly, or a parent night.

Note how special effects enrich the following rendition of the Gettysburg Address. The results is a performance with features of RT, like scripts in hand and focus on voice interpretation; but there are also characteristics of drama, like gestures and movements. The performance has both ear-and eye-gate appeal for the audience. Simultaneously it requires deep conceptual understanding on the part of the performers.

Director's Information

Gettysburg Address
By Abraham Lincoln adapted for Readers Theatre
6 Readers: READER 1,2,3,4 (R1,R2,R3,R4); INTERPRETER 1,2 (IN1,IN2)
(See Chapter 12 for a copy of the performers' script.)

Entrance: The Readers enter in the following order from the rear of the room:
R1, R2, R3, R4, IN1, IN2.
Positioning: R1, R2, R3, R4 are full-back. IN1 and IN2 take the full front
position. Note diagram below.

Up Stage Right	Up Stage Center	Up Stage Left
Center Stage Right R1　R1　R3 R4	Center Stage　　IN2	Center Stage Left IN1
Down Stage Right	Down Stage Center	Down Stage Left

(Front of the Stage)

Focus: Off stage.
Levels: All on same level.
Props: None.
Scripts as Props: As seems natural to the readers.
Sound effects: None.
Stands/lecterns: None.
Voicing: See bold-faced type in the script.
Exit: After the presentation, the readers take a slight bow and leave the stage
DSL in the reverse order of entering.

Gettysburg Address

By Abraham Lincoln adapted for Readers Theatre
6 Readers: Readers 1-4, Interpreter 1,2

Prologue

INTERPRETER 1: The battle of Gettysburg,
INTERPRETER 2: the turning point of the Civil War,
INTERPRETER 1: occurred in July 1863.
INTERPRETER 2: The grounds were consecrated
INTERPRETER 1: for a new cemetery in November of that same year.
INTERPRETER 2: Edward Everett was asked to give the principal oration.
INTERPRETER 1: He was a noted preacher,
INTERPRETER 2: a professor of Greek,
INTERPRETER 1: a United States Senator,
INTERPRETER 2: a Secretary of State,
INTERPRETER 1: a president of Harvard.
INTERPRETER 2: Abraham Lincoln was also asked to give
INTERPRETER 1: a few appropriate remarks.
INTERPRETER 2: He attended school less than one year. He was
INTERPRETER 1: a log splitter,
INTERPRETER 2: a lawyer,
INTERPRETER 1: a representative,
INTERPRETER 2: the President of the United States.
INTERPRETER 1: Everett's long oration was given by heart.
INTERPRETER 2: Lincoln's short address was given from the heart.
INTERPRETER 1: And now the Gettysburg Address by Abraham Lincoln.
IN1 and IN2 quickly take the CSR position and lower their heads.
READERS 1–4 face full front.

The Address

READER 1: Fourscore and seven years ago
ALL READERS: our fathers
IN 1 and IN 2 left their heads.
INTERPRETER 1: That is 70 years!
INTERPRETER 2: They were English, Germans, Scots, Dutch, Germans, and on and on.
READER 2: brought forth on this continent a new nation,
READER 4:conceived in liberty
READER 2:and dedicated to the proposition
ALL READERS: *Solemnly.*

that all men are created equal.

READERS 1,4:Now we are engaged in a great civil war,

Loudly and with feeling for the next two lines.

READER 4:testing whether that nation

READER 3:or any nation

READER 4:so conceived

READER 1: *Solemnly.*

and so dedicated can long endure.

READERS 2,4:We are met on a great battlefield of that war.

READER 1,3:We have come to dedicate a portion of that field

READER 3:as a final resting-place

READER 1:for those who here gave their lives

READER 2:that that nation might live.

READER 3:It is altogether fitting

READER 4: *Pause.*

and proper that we should do this.

READER 1:But in a larger sense,

READERS 1,3:we cannot dedicate,

READERS 1,3,2:we cannot consecrate,

READERS 1,3,2,4:we cannot hallow this ground.

READER 2:The brave men,

READER 3:living and dead

READER 1:who struggled here

READER 4:have consecrated it far above

READER 2:our poor power to add or detract.

READER 3: *Pause.*

The world will little note

READER 2:nor long remember what we say here,

READER 1:but it can never forget

READERS 3,4: *Upbeat voice.*

what they did here.

READER 2: It is for us the living

READER 4: rather to be dedicated here to the unfinished work

READER 2: which they who fought

READER 3: here have thus far so nobly advanced.

READER 4: It is rather for us

READER 1: to be here dedicated to the great task remaining before us—

READER 2: That from these honored dead

READER 3: we take increased devotion
READER 4: *Pause and then firmly say.*
THAT CAUSE for which they gave the last full measure of devotion—
READER 2: That we here highly resolve
READER 1: *Shake heads.*
that these dead
ALL READERS: shall not have died in vain.

READERS 1,4: *With heads up and proclaiming.*
That this nation
READER 4: under God shall have a new birth of freedom,
READER 2: and that government
READER 4: of the people,
READER 3: by the people,
READER 1: for the people
ALL READERS: shall not perish from the earth.

A FINAL WORD

The purpose of RT is effective interpretation. Every decision about adding features beyond expressive use of the voice should be carefully weighed by asking these questions: Does this add to the learning of the content? Does this add to the message? If special voice inflections, movements, positioning, sound effects, props, or simple costumes make the experience more meaningful for both performers and audience, consider incorporating them. If they reduce academic learning time or detract from your instructional goals, it is probably better to save these efforts for your drama club.

After a performance that has been enhanced with special effects, we always ask the students what they will most remember from the experience. If they talk about the ideas within the script—either content knowledge or story theme—we know the enrichments have been appropriate.

Teachers with no drama training can guide their students to prepare interesting, educational presentations through RT. When students have had extensive experience with this format, teachers can relinquish the task of producing a dramatic presentation to the class. The students become not just actors, but also writers, prop managers, and directors. It takes virtually no outlay of money to design a powerful RT. Learning arises, not from expensive materials of equipment, but from the creative minds of students.

IV

Readers Theatre Resources
for the Classroom

8

Preparing Lesson Plans for Effective Use of Readers Theatre

Some teachers see Readers Theatre (RT) as an add-on, an enjoyable break from instruction. We argue that this format should be viewed, not as a release from, but rather as an essential component of, concept and skill development.

Included in this chapter are examples of Readers Theatre scripts used as instructional tools for:

- Science and Language Arts (Kindergarten and above)

- Mathematics and Language Arts (Grade 5 and above)

- Language Arts (Grade 5 and above)

- Chemistry (Grade 9 and above)

- History (Grade 5 and above)

To ensure that we are addressing our teaching goals, we pose several questions each time we prepare lessons that incorporate RT.

- What concepts or content am I trying to impart through this piece?

- What objectives/standards am I addressing?

- Where does this best fit into the instructional flow; i.e., should I use this piece to introduce, explore, or extend students' understandings?

- How will I be sure that all students are involved in this experience; i.e., how should roles and responsibilities be determined?

- How will I gather evidence about individual students' levels of progress toward meeting the objective?

To facilitate this process we have developed a planning grid.

Concepts or content	
Objectives/standards	
Placement of Readers Theatre within instruction	
Student involvement	
Evidence (Assessment)	

In this chapter are examples from our own experiences to show how an RT script can serve as a central component of focused instruction. You will note that the objectives on the grids are based on the national standards. State or local curricula may use slightly different wording, but are usually linked to these nationwide guidelines.

We have provided a blank form, in hopes that you will find it helpful. If it does not fit your needs exactly, feel free to make modifications to suit your own style.

LESSON PLANNING GRID

Concepts or content	
Objectives/standards	
Placement of Readers Theatre within instruction	
Student involvement	
Evidence (Assessment)	

EXAMPLE 1

Science and Language Arts
Activity: Nature Walk and Patterned Talk

Concept/Content	Colors found in nature Patterns use in language
Objective(s)	• Recognize and distinguish similarities and differences in species. (Science) • Apply knowledge of sentence structure. (Language Arts)
Placement of Readers Theatre within instruction	• Use after a Nature Walk, during which children collect ideas for creating the Readers Theatre.
Student Involvement	• Post 5 colored card (red, green, blue, yellow, brown) in separate areas of the room. • Tell students that each of them will be looking for things of one of these colors during a Nature Walk. • At random, give each child a red, green, blue, yellow, or brown card on which is written this cloze sentence: I am _____. • Take children on silent Nature Walk to look for things of their individual colors. • In the classroom, have children move to the places in the room where their colors are posted, and take down the colored cards. • Lead group reading of two cloze sentences from the board: I am _____. We are _____. Explain that each child is to fill in the first sentence with something he saw of his color. Group members are to chat with each other to make each sentence is different. Each child in the group will read his/her finished sentence 1. Then the whole group will say, "We are__" and the class will guess the color to cloze the second sentence. Give an example using a color other than red, green, blue, yellow, or brown. • Allow planning and practicing time. • Call on groups to share, with the class finishing each set. Children show cards to check the class guess.

Evidence (Assessment)	• Individual students' choices of nature items by colors (Science) • Individual students' sentence structure in making completions (Language Arts)

Following is an example of a RT prepared by a kindergarten class.

Nature Walk
Entire class

READER 1: I am a flower.
READER 2: I am a berry.
READER 3: I am Mrs. C.'s dress. *
READER 4: I am a prickly pear.
AUDIENCE: We are [RED].

READER 5: I am a leaf.
READER 6: I am grass.
READER 7: I am a bush.
AUDIENCE: We are [GREEN].

READER 8: I am the sky.
READER 9: I am a bird.
READER 10: I am a puddle.
AUDIENCE: We are [BLUE].

READER 11: I am a dog.
READER 12: I am bark.
READER 13: I am a bird.
READER 14: I am a cloud.**
AUDIENCE: We are [BROWN].

READER 15: I am the sun.
READER 16: I am a flower.
READER 17: I am a stripe on a bee.
AUDIENCE: We are [YELLOW].

*At the close of the lesson we reviewed every item, and the child himself decided his choice was <u>not</u> a <u>nature</u> item.

**This was a dust cloud on a windy day, giving an opportunity for a good science discussion.

EXAMPLE 2

Mathematics and Language Arts
Activity: Circle Pun Fun and Calculation of a Circle's Area

Concepts or content	Circumference, diameter, radius, pi, area and their relationships Terms with different meanings in different subject areas
Objectives/standards	Define geometric terms. (Mathematics) Calculate the area of a circle. (Mathematics) Identify morphemes, homophones, and words with multiple meanings. (Language Arts)
Placement of Readers Theatre within instruction	Use as an introduction to the mathematics topic and as reinforcement following instruction.

Student involvement	• To introduce the concept, present the RT as a performance by two teachers (or a teacher and an advanced student). Note students' responses; whether they catch the humor will indicate their levels of prior knowledge about circle-related terms.
	• To teach the math concept, distribute manipulatives.
	Ask each student to:
	  - make a circle of graph paper; and
	  - count the number of squares within the circle, adding the partial square to obtain the area.
	Guide the class to an understanding of the formula for calculating the area of a circle.

	• To further explore the concept, select two students to prepare and present the RT. (You may opt to divide the script into sections, assign pairs, or provide time for repeated performances by different groups in order to involve more students.) Divide the class into cooperative groups. Distribute copies of the RT, one per person, on which students are to underline the plays on words included in the RT. During full-class sharing, have students explain the morpheme, homophones, and multiple meanings of words used in the plays on words.
Evidence (Assessment)	Responses to deliveries of and discussions about the RT (Mathematics and Language Arts) Quiz on the definitions of circle-related terms (Mathematics) Individual solving of area problems (Mathematics) Lists of plays on words (Language Arts)

How Big is That Pi?

by Randy Nomura
2 Readers
(See the complete reproducible script in Chapter 11.)

Reader 1: The area of a circle is pi r squared.
Reader 2: Pie are squared?
Reader 1: Yes, pi r squared!
Reader 2: But, I thought pies are round?
Reader 1: Pies are round!
Reader 2: But you said pie are squared!
Reader 1: Not pie are squared! Pi r squared!
Reader 2: Pie are squared?
Reader 1: Yes. the area of a circle is pi r squared!

...

Reader 1: Distance across the circle. Diameter!
Reader 2: Is that equal to two meters?
Reader 1: Two meters?
Reader 2: Yes, two meters! Doesn't di mean two?
Reader 1: Well, I guess it would if the circle was big enough!

...

Reader 2: My units are pies!
Reader 1: Not are pies! Pi r squared!
Reader 2: I get it!!! The pies that are squared are two meters across and have a round crust like the middle area of approximately 3.14 circles! I'm so smart!
Reader 1: I'm hungry!

EXAMPLE 3

Language Arts
Activity: The Power of Prepositional Phrases

Concepts or content*	Prepositions and prepositional phrases
Objectives/standards	Identify prepositional phrases within a story. Explain functions of prepositional phrases.
Placement of Readers Theatre within instruction	Use as an introduction to the topic and/or as an extension of understanding after instruction.

Student involvement	If using as an introduction, follow these steps: 1. Pre-assign parts to four solo readers, who practice and then present the RT. 2. Distribute copies of the complete script (with prepositions) to all students. As a class, identify all prepositional phrases; students mark them on their copies. 3. Divide the class into cooperative groups; assign each an equal number of phrases to prepare as pantomimes. 4. Randomly call on groups to act out their phrases. Ask the class to identify each. 5. As a class, list the functions of prepositional phrases. 6. Assign as individual homework labeling the function of each prepositional phrase in the RT. 7. Divide the class into cooperative groups and distribute copies of the incomplete scripts (without prepositional phrases). Allow for creativity, but specify that each blank must contain a prepositional phrase that would make sense, i.e., that fits one of the functions listed in step 5. 8. Call on each group to present its RT to the full class. If time is a factor, each team may share with one other. 9. Assign four students to read the original complete script as students follow on their own copies. As a class compare the original with the student versions. If using for reinforcement only, begin at step 7.
Evidence (Assessment)	Responses during steps 2, 4, 5, 8, and 9.

*Note that this script would be particularly appropriate if the class were studying causes of European exploration during the 16th Century.

Sir Francis Drake
(with prepositions)
4 Readers: READER 1,2,3,4
(See the complete reproducible script in Chapter 9.)

READER 1: He won the sea

READER 2: as a heritage for England.
READER 3: Frances Drake,
READER 4: son of a clergyman,
READER 3: an apprentice on slave trade to the New World.
READER 1: As he grew older
READER 4: he turned to Privateering.
READER 3: (A polite term for stealing.)
...
READER 4: to sail around the world
READER 2: capturing many prizes on the way
READER 4: and returning laden with treasure.
READER 2: As a reward Queen Elizabeth knighted him
READER 1: Now he was...Sir Francis Drake!
...
READER 4: the mistress of the seas for three centuries!
READER 2: Sir Frances Drake!
READER 3: Born on land in England.
READER 1: Died at sea in the West Indies.

Sir Francis Drake
(without prepositions)

4 Readers: READER or GROUP1,2,3,4

READER 1: He won the sea
READER 2: as a heritage _____
READER 3: Frances Drake,
READER 4: son _____,
READER 3: an apprentice _____ _____.
READER 1: As he grew older
READER 4: he turned _____.
READER 3: (A polite term _____.)
...
READER 4: to sail _____.
READER 2: capturing many prizes _____
READER 4: and returning laden _____.
READER 2: As a reward Queen Elizabeth knighted him
READER 1: Now he was...Sir Francis Drake!

...
READER 1: and made England
READER 4: the mistress _____ _____.
READER 2: Sir Frances Drake!
READER 3: Born _____ _____.
READER 1: Died _____ _____.

EXAMPLE 4

Chemistry Class
Topic: Oxidation and Reduction
Grades: 10-12

Concepts or content	Oxidation, reduction, chemical and physical change
Objectives/standards	Define and identify examples of oxidation and reduction. Define and identify examples of chemical reactions and electron transfer. Differentiate between physical and chemical change.
Placement of Readers Theatre within instruction	Use as an introduction to the topic and, after instruction, as a summary to reinforce the concepts.
Student involvement	Distribute copies of the RT and perform; the teacher serves as the reader and the class as the audience. After instruction, students individually identify certain aspects of the reading as oxidation, reduction, chemical and physical change by marking in the script where each occurs.
Evidence (Assessment)	Marked scripts. Follow-up quiz

Fire, Fire, Fire

2 Readers: READER, AUDIENCE
(See the complete reproducible script in Chapter 10.)

AUDIENCE: Fire! Fire! Fire!
READER: The ultimate in chemical change!

AUDIENCE: Will it change me?

READER: Yes, into something new.

AUDIENCE: When you are through with me, will I look different?

READER: And smell and taste different,

AUDIENCE: melt at a different temperature?

READER: and boil at a different temperature. You will be different.

AUDIENCE: I am fire. I am good

READER: and bad at times.

AUDIENCE: I am red

…

AUDIENCE: Let's start a fire to cook.

READER: While you are cooking I'll have an order of hash browns and two eggs easy over.

AUDIENCE: In the early day they worked very hard to get me started.

READER: By hitting rocks together

AUDIENCE: or rubbing sticks together.

READER: Today we just strike a match.

…

READER: In a forest fire you would wish for no air!

AUDIENCE: With people one never knows either.

READER: It's freezing in here.

AUDIENCE: They light me.

READER: Hey buddy, got a match?

AUDIENCE: They feed me.

READER: Put another log on.

AUDIENCE: But then they forget about me.

READER: Did you turn the fire off?

AUDIENCE: No, why?

…

READER: Need to call 911 again!

AUDIENCE: Use me,

READER: but don't abuse you.

AUDIENCE: I am fire,

READER: a chemical changer.

AUDIENCE: I don't really understand.

READER: Chemistry?

AUDIENCE: Chemistry, yes! But people—naw!

READER: The end of this Readers Theatre, but not of fire.

EXAMPLE 5

History
Activity: Justice for a Woman?

Concepts or content	Women's issues
Objectives/standards	Trace the struggle of women and their issues throughout history.
Placement of Readers Theatre within instruction	Use as an introduction to the topic.
Student involvement	• Establish groups of seven. Assign parts prior to class, allowing time for practice. (If class size is not divisible by seven, pairs of readers my be assigned to any role.) • Call on each group to perform. During each presentation, each audience member is to listen for and jot down a word or phrase particularly well delivered to highlight the injustice issue. • Collect these notes; grade and return them for use during a sharing session. As a follow-up activity assign short articles about significant women who have advanced the cause of women's rights. These will be analyzed per criteria given in class.
Evidence (Assessment)	Expressiveness during class presentations Notes on RT scripts Analyses during follow-up activity

Susanna from the Hebrew Tradition

7 Readers: READER 1, 2, 3; ELDER 1, 2; SUSANNA, DANIEL
(See the complete reproducible script in Chapter 12.)

READER 1: Susanna was very beautiful.
READER 2: She feared the Lord,
READER 3: had righteous parents, and
READER 2: was taught according to the law of Moses.
READER 1: She was married to a very rich man,

...

READER 3: One day the two Elders said,

ELDER 1 & 2: Let us go home, for it is mealtime.

READER 1 They parted from each other

READER 3: but came back to the garden from different ways,

ELDER 1: Why are you going back?

ELDER 2: Why are <u>you</u> going back?

...

READER 1: with her children

READER 3: with her kindred.

READER 1: with her beauty

READER 2: with her refinement.

READER 3: with her veil.

ELDER 2: Take off the veil!

READER 2: Her family wept.

READER 1: Her friends wept.

READER 2: Susanna wept as she said,

...

ELDER 1: Under an evergreen oak.

DANIEL: Very well, you both lied against your own heads. The angel of God has received the sentence from God and will immediately cut you in two.

READER 2: And they rose against the Elders

READER 1: and they did to them as they had

READER 2: wickedly planned to do to Susanna.

READER 1: They put them to death in accordance with the law of Moses.

READER 2: And so the question can be asked today, in fact, especially today,

READER 3: if there is no justice for women,

READER 2: can there be justice for anyone?

9

Language Arts—Sample Scripts

It is probably safe to say that any Readers Theatre (RT) in this book could be listed under the language arts heading! In this chapter you will find a variety of scripts we have designated as language arts scripts, but many could certainly be used in other subjects. Similarly, scripts in Chapter 10-12 may fit better into a language arts lesson than in the content areas we suggest. At first we tried to divide the scripts by grade levels, but we soon came to realize that they could be shared with a wide range of age groups. Often it is how the script is introduced that determines whether students are comfortable and would benefit by the reading. Feel free to use the RTs in Chapter 9-12 wherever they will best enhance student learning. You are the professional who will make these choices based on your curriculum and the needs of your students.

The list below gives an overview of the content and instructional focus of each script included in this chapter. At the end of the chapter is a section entitled **Presentational End Notes**. They contain our suggestions for ways these Readers Theatres could be used in the classroom.

- Aesop's "The Lion, the Wolf, and the Fox"—Demonstrates the key features of a fable with a moral.

- Cinderella—Stimulates discussion on the timely theme of family relationships, addressing sibling rivalry, the challenges of a blended family, development of self-esteem and the importance of kindness to others.

- Friends, An Old African Tale—Stimulates discussion on the theme of friendship, while also demonstrating the characteristics of a trickster tale.

- Georgie Porgie—Gives students practice with verbs and their gerunds.

- Goldilocks—Allows students to experiment with the predictable patterns in this familiar tale.

- Homographic Pronunciation Fun—Helps students anchor the pronunciations of homographs. The pattern is established, but should serve as a "starter," to which students add their own segments.

- Homophonic Spelling Fun—Helps students anchor the spellings of homophones. The pattern is established, but should serve as a "starter," to which students add their own segments.

- House That Jack Built—Gives an excellent opportunity for students to feel the cadence of the English language.

- Humpty Dumpty—Provides predictability of word usage to help build fluency.

- Into the Forest—Focuses on locational prepositions and past tense verbs.

- Jack—Requires making inferences from references to traditional literature.

- Multiple Meaning Fun—Helps students recognize various meanings for words that are spelled and pronounced the same. The pattern is established, but should serve as a "starter," to which students add their own segments.

- My First Friend—Shows the power of effective word choices to enhance a theme by expressing the feelings many students experience as they cast about for acceptance.

- Radio Time—Demonstrates the connection between prediction and twists in a plot. It can also lead to analysis of words with different meanings in different contexts/subject areas.

- Sewing—Includes clever uses of words with multiple meanings.

- Three Little Kittens—Provides an opportunity for even the emerging readers to be successful.

- Three Little Pigs—Gives students opportunity to build fluency through repeated patterns, but also to enjoy a surprise ending to this familiar tale.

- Three Wishes—Introduces critical thinking by establishing an environmental theme, and then demonstrating emotional versus intellectual problem solving skills.

Aesop's "The Lion, the Wolf and the Fox"
By Jennifer Oliverio
5 Readers: NARRATORS 1-3, WOLF, FOX

NARRATOR 1: A very old lion lay sick in his cave.

NARRATOR 2: All of the animals

NARRATOR 3: came to pay their respects to their king,

NARRATOR 2: except for the fox.

NARRATOR 1: The wolf,

NARRATOR 3: being a sly creature,

NARRATOR 2: accused the fox in front of the lion.

NARRATOR 1: The wolf cried,

WOLF: The fox has no respect for you, your Majesty.

NARRATOR 3: What? Growled the lion.

WOLF: That's why he didn't show.

NARRATOR 2: Just as the wolf was saying,

WOLF: That's why he didn't show.

NARRATOR 1: the fox arrived,

NARRATOR 3: and overheard the wolf's lie.

NARRATOR 2: When the lion saw the fox

NARRATOR 1: he roared with rage at him.

NARRATOR 3: But the fox managed to say,

FOX: Your Majesty,

NARRATOR 2: The lion roared again.

FOX: I was away because I searched far and wide to find a remedy for ill-ness,...

NARRATOR 3: The lion roared again even more loudly.

FOX: and I have found one.

NARRATOR 1: The lion demanded to know what cure he had found,

NARRATOR 2: and the fox replied,

FOX: You must skin a wolf alive and wrap his skin around you while it is still warm.

NARRATOR 3: So the lion ordered the wolf

NARRATOR 1: to be taken away at once

NARRATOR 2: and skinned alive.

NARRATOR 3: As the wolf was being carried away,

NARRATOR 2: the fox turned to him with a smile, a sly smile,

NARRATOR 3: and said,

FOX: You should have spoken well of me to His Majesty rather than ill.
NARRATOR 1: The moral of this fable is:
NARRATOR 2: If you speak ill of someone,
NARRATOR 1: you yourself will fall into a trap.

Cinderella

8 Readers: NARRATORS 1,2; SISTERS 1,2; CINDERELLA, FAIRY
GODPERSON, FOOTMAN, PRINCE

SISTER 1: Cinderella!

SISTER 2: Sweep the floor.

SISTER 1: Cinderella!

SISTER 2: Wash the dishes.

SISTER 1: Cinderella!

SISTER 2: Make the beds.

SISTER 1: Cinderella!

SISTER 2: Clean the windows.

SISTER 1: Cinderella!

SISTER 2: Cook the food.

SISTER 1: Bring the wood.

SISTER 2: Light the fire.

SISTER 1: Scrub the floors.

SISTER 2: Work, work, work!

CINDERELLA: Those are my stepsisters!

NARRATOR 1: Each morning

NARRATOR 2: they gave Cinderella her chores in their sweetest voices.

SISTER 1: Cinderella!

CINDERELLA: They want me to do this.

SISTER 2: Cinderella!

CINDERELLA: They want me to do that.

SISTER 1: Cinderella!

CINDERELLA: They want me to do this and that.

NARRATOR 1: In the afternoon

NARRATOR 2: the stepsisters spent their time

NARRATOR 1: trying to make themselves beautiful

NARRATOR 2: which of course was an endless and hopeless task—

NARRATOR 1: If you know what I mean.

SISTER 1,2: Cinderella! Cinderella!

CINDERELLA: Here we go again.

SISTER 1: Brush my hair!

SISTER 2: Cinderella!

SISTER 1: Iron my dress.

SISTER 2: Cinderella!

SISTER 1: Tie my bow.
SISTER 2: Powder my nose.
SISTER 1: Zip my zipper.
SISTER 2: Button my buttons.
SISTER 1: Bring by shoes.
SISTER 2: Hem my dress.
SISTER 1: Find my makeup.
SISTER 1,2: Cinderella! Cinderella!
NARRATOR 1: Poor Cinderella!
NARRATOR 2: But I am here to tell you
NARRATOR 1: that no matter what the stepsisters did or what Cinderella did
NARRATOR 2: to make them look nice they were still were very ug—
NARRATOR 1: Let's not use that word!
NARRATOR 2: One day a letter came to the house.
FOOTMAN: All of you are invited to a ball at the palace.
Both SISTERS: Yes, we will come.
CINDERELLA: Am I invited?
FOOTMAN: Yes, everyone is invited.
SISTER 2: She has too much work to do.
CINDERELLA: But I would like to go—
SISTER 1: You are too busy getting us ready.
CINDERELLA: I still would like to go.
SISTER 1,2: No, no, no.
SISTER 2: You have work, work, work to do.
FOOTMAN: Everyone, everyone is invited to the ball.
NARRATOR 2: The day of the ball came.
NARRATOR 1: The stepsisters kept Cinderella very busy in the morning.
NARRATOR 2: Cinderella, Cinderella, Cinderella!
CINDERELLA: Won't they ever quit?
SISTER 1: Make the beds.
SISTER 2: Sweep the floor.
SISTER 1: Wash the dishes.
SISTER 2: Make the beds.
SISTER 1: Clean the windows.
SISTER 2: Cook the food.
SISTER 1: Do this.
SISTER 2: Do that.
CINDERELLA: Yes, and do this and that.

NARRATOR 1: In the afternoon

NARRATOR 2: the stepsisters spent their time trying to make themselves beautiful.

NARRATOR 1: which of course was an endless and hopeless task—

NARRATOR 2: If you know what I mean.

SISTER 1: Cinderella! I must get ready for the ball.

SISTER 2: Cinderella! I must get ready for the ball.

NARRATOR 1: So the sisters,

NARRATOR 2: again in their sweetest voices, asked her to—

SISTER 1: Brush my hair.

SISTER 2: Iron my dress.

SISTER 1: Tie my bow.

SISTER 2: Powder my nose.

SISTER 1: Zip my zipper.

SISTER 2: Button my buttons.

SISTER 1: Shine my shoes.

SISTER 2: Hem my dress.

SISTER 1: Find my makeup.

NARRATOR 1: And so it was all day that Cinderella was very busy.

CINDERELLA: I have been so busy that I have had no time to get ready for the ball.

NARRATOR 2: But her stepsisters were ready,

NARRATOR 1: well as ready as they would ever be—

NARRATOR 2: If you know what I mean.

NARRATOR 1: Cinderella sat on a box by the fire

NARRATOR 2: and among her tears said,

CINDERELLA: I wish I could go to the ball.

FAIRY GODPERSON: You shall go to the ball!

NARRATOR 2: It was the voice of the Fairy Godmother or was it the Fairy Godfather?

CINDERELLA: You surprised me!

FAIRY GODPERSON: You are going to the palace ball!

CINDERELLA: But I have no way to get there.

FAIRY GODPERSON: Bring me a pumpkin

NARRATOR 1: which was turned immediately into a coach.

CINDERELLA: But I need horses to pull the coach.

FAIRY GODPERSON: Bring me four white mice

NARRATOR 1: which were turned immediately into four white horses.

CINDERELLA: But I have no one to drive the coach.
FAIRY GODPERSON: Bring me two lizards
NARRATOR 1: which were turned into a driver and a footman.
CINDERELLA: But I have only rags to wear to the ball.
NARRATOR 2: At this the Fairy Godperson waved the magic wand
NARRATOR 1: and Cinderella was dressed in a beautiful gown
NARRATOR 2: and dainty glass slippers.
CINDERELLA: Now I am ready for the ball!
NARRATOR 1:The Fairy Godperson did give one warning.
CINDERELLA: I must leave before the clock strikes twelve?
FAIRY GODPERSON: Yes, at twelve everything will change back again.
CINDERELLA: Oh, thank you, thank you! I will remember.
NARRATOR 1: At the ball Cinderella danced
NARRATOR 2: and danced with the Prince
NARRATOR 1: while the stepsisters looked on.
CINDERELLA: I am so happy I could dance all night.
NARRATOR 1: In fact she was so happy
NARRATOR 2: that she lost track of time.
CINDERELLA: The Fairy Godperson forgot to give me a watch!
NARRATOR 2: She heard the palace clock begin
NARRATOR 1: to strike the chimes of midnight.
CINDERELLA: One, two, three, four…oh no.
NARRATOR 1: Oh, yes.
NARRATOR 2: It was twelve o'clock.
CINDERELLA: I must go!
NARRATOR 1: But the prince said,
PRINCE: No.
NARRATOR 2: In spite of the prince's 'No' she ran from the palace…
PRINCE: Stop, stop.
NARRATOR 2: …down the palace steps losing one of her glass slippers ran Cinderella,
NARRATOR 1: just as the clock struck twelve.
FAIRY GODPERSON: My warning is now coming true.
NARRATOR 1: The coach did became a pumpkin,
NARRATOR 2: the white horses became white mice and ran away,
NARRATOR 1: and the driver and footman became lizards
NARRATOR 2: and hid under a rock.
CINDERELLA: My clothes are turned to rags.

NARRATOR 1: For Cinderella it was a long and sad walk home
NARRATOR 2: carrying the pumpkin.
NARRATOR 1: Back at the palace the Prince had found the glass slipper
NARRATOR 2: and ordered his footman to find the owner.
PRINCE: Once you find the girl, I will marry her.
NARRATOR 1: Naturally every girl in the kingdom
NARRATOR 2 thought the slipper would fit her foot.
NARRATOR 1: The stepsisters had their try at putting it on.
NARRATOR 2: But the footman only laughed
NARRATOR 1: even though the stepsisters painfully said,
SISTER 1,2: This is a perfect fit!
NARRATOR 2: The footman had tried everyone in the kingdom
NARRATOR 1: and since the shoe didn't fit
NARRATOR 2: no one was to wear it.
NARRATOR 1: Just then Cinderella walked into the room with mops and brooms
NARRATOR 2: with buckets and rags,
NARRATOR 1: with towels and dishes.
NARRATOR 2: The footman said,
FOOTMAN: Please try on the slipper.
SISTER 2: Don't waste your time.
FOOTMAN: The Prince said everyone—
SISTER 1: The Prince would never marry her!
FOOTMAN: The Prince said everyone should try on the shoe.
NARRATOR 1: It fit Cinderella perfectly!
BOTH SISTERS: Oh no—
NARRATOR 2: And the Stepsisters fainted away.
NARRATOR 1: But I am here to tell you that they were at the wedding
NARRATOR 2: of the Prince and Cinderella, but not looking very happy,
NARRATOR 1: because when they got home, they would have to—
SISTER 1: Sweep the floor.
SISTER 2: Wash the dishes.
SISTER 1: Make the beds.
SISTER 2: Clean the windows.
SISTER 1: Cook the food.
SISTER 2: Do this.
SISTER 1: Do that.
SISTERS 1,2: Do this and that.

SISTER 2: Brush hair.
SISTER 1: Iron dresses.
SISTER 2: Tie bows.
SISTER 1: Powder noses.
SISTER 2: Zip zippers.
SISTER 1: Button buttons.
SISTER 2: Shine shoes.
SISTER 1: Hem dresses
NARRATOR 2: and on and on.

NARRATOR 1: The sisters learned a big lesson!
NARRATOR 2: You should be careful how you treat other people
NARRATOR 1: because the shoe you make other people walk in,
NARRATOR 2: you may have to wear yourself.
NARRATOR 1: As for Cinderella, she liked the old saying—
CINDERELLA: If the shoe fits, wear it!

Friends—An African Folk Tale

9 Readers: VOICES 1-5; TORTOISE, RHINOCEROS, ELEPHANT, HARE

VOICE 1: Long ago

VOICE 2: Tortoise bragged,

TORTOISE: I am the greatest of all creatures!

VOICE 3: But rhinoceros disagreed,

RHINO: I am the greatest of all creatures!

VOICE 2: Elephant argued,

ELEPHANT: I am the greatest of all creatures!

VOICE 4: Hare insisted,

HARE: You are all great and must be friends.

VOICE 5: But Tortoise, Rhinoceros, and Elephant scoffed.

TORTOISE, RHINO, ELEPHANT: Never!

VOICE 3: As time passed,

VOICE 1: Tortoise began to think about Hare's words.

VOICE 4: One day,

VOICE 2: he visited Rhinoceros and said,

TORTOISE: Rhinoceros, we both think we are the greatest.

VOICE 5: Rhinoceros boasted,

RHINO: I am the greatest of all creatures.

VOICE 4: Tortoise spoke calmly:

TORTOISE: I propose a contest.

VOICE 1: Rhinoceros smiled.

RHINO: That sounds fair.

VOICE 3: Tortoise suggested the rules:

TORTOISE: Here is a long vine. We will each take one end and pull.

VOICE 5: Rhinoceros smiled a sly smile.

RHINO: That sounds fair.

TORTOISE: If you pull me to your side,

RHINO: I am the greatest.

TORTOISE: If I pull you to my side, I am the greatest.

RHINO: That sounds fair.

TORTOISE: If the vine breaks before I pull you to my side of the wadi,

RHINO: or I pull you to my side of the wadi,

TORTOISE: we will declare ourselves equals,

RHINO: That sounds fair.

TORTOISE: ...and therefore friends.

RHINO: That sounds fair.

TORTOISE: Let us get a good night's rest first.

RHINO: You will need it, you puny creature.

TORTOISE: As soon as the sun rises, I will give three small tugs on the vine.

RHINO: Meaning "begin"?

TORTOISE: Yes. Pull as hard as you can.

RHINO: That sounds fair.

VOICES 4: Tortoise turned to leave.

TORTOISE: Rest well and good luck, Friend.

RHINO: You are the one who needs the luck, puny one, and DON'T CALL ME FRIEND!

VOICE 5: Tortoise left,

VOICE 2: taking one end of the vine with him.

VOICE 4: He scrambled through the foliage,

VOICE 1: to the other side of the wadi,

VOICE 5: and through more foliage.

VOICE 3: There he visited Elephant.

VOICE 1: He said,

TORTOISE: Elephant, we both think we are the greatest.

VOICES 5: Elephant boasted,

ELEPHANT: I am the greatest of all creatures.

VOICES 4: Tortoise spoke calmly:

TORTOISE: I propose a contest.

VOICES 1: Elephant smiled.

ELEPHANT: That sounds fair.

VOICE 3: Tortoise once again gave the rules:

TORTOISE: Here is a long vine. We will each take one end and pull.

VOICE 5: Elephant smiled a sly smile.

ELEPHANT: That sounds fair.

TORTOISE: If you pull me to your side,

ELEPHANT: I am the greatest.

TORTOISE: If I pull you to my side, I am the greatest.

ELEPHANT: That sounds fair.

TORTOISE: If the vine breaks before I pull you to my side of the wadi,

ELEPHANT: or I pull you to my side of the wadi,

TORTOISE: we will declare ourselves equals,

ELEPHANT: That sounds fair.

TORTOISE: ...and therefore friends.

ELEPHANT: That sounds fair.

TORTOISE: Let us get a good night's rest first.

ELEPHANT: You will need it, you puny creature.

TORTOISE: As soon as the sun rises, I will give three small tugs on the vine.

ELEPHANT: Meaning "begin"?

TORTOISE: Yes. Pull as hard as you can.

ELEPHANT: That sounds fair.

VOICES 4: Tortoise turned to leave.

TORTOISE: Rest well and good luck, Friend.

ELEPHANT: You are the one who needs the luck, puny one, and DON'T CALL ME FRIEND!

VOICE 5: Tortoise left,

VOICE 2: following the vine back to the middle of the wadi.

VOICE 1: In the morning,

VOICE 2: as the sun began to rise,

VOICE 4: Tortoise gave three quick tugs on the vine.

VOICE 5: Immediately, the vine became taut

VOICE 2: as the rhinoceros

VOICE 4: and the elephant

VOICES 2 & 4: began to pull,

VOICE 2: and pull,

VOICE 4: and pull.

VOICE 3: Tortoise smiled a sly smile

VOICE 5: as he watched the vine

VOICE 3: go a bit this way,

VOICE 5: and a bit that way,

VOICE 3: and a bit this way,

VOICE 5: and a bit that way,

VOICE 2: always remaining taut.

VOICE 1: After a while,

VOICE 4: Tortoise smiled a sly smile,

VOICE 2: made a quick stab

VOICE 5: with his very sharp claw,

VOICE 3: and snapped the vine in two.

VOICE 1: From each side of the wadi he heard

VOICE 4: a huge bump.

VOICE 1: Tortoise waddled to see Rhinoceros,

VOICE 3: who sat rubbing his bottom

VOICE 4: and looking puzzled.

VOICE 5: Tortoise smiled a sly smile and said,

TORTOISE: I could not beat you.

VOICES 1: Rhinoceros replied in a stunned voice,

RHINO: I could not beat you.

TORTOISE: Are we equals?

RHINO: Yes, we are equals.

TORTOISE: And friends?

RHINO: Yes, friends.

VOICE 1: Tortoise waddled to the other side of the wadi

VOICE 5: to see Elephant,

VOICE 3: who sat rubbing his bottom

VOICE 4: and looking puzzled.

VOICE 5: Tortoise smiled a sly smile and said,

TORTOISE: I could not beat you.

VOICE 1: Elephant replied in a stunned voice,

ELEPHANT: I could not beat you.

TORTOISE: Are we equals?

ELEPHANT: Yes, we are equals.

TORTOISE: And friends?

ELEPHANT: Yes, friends.

VOICE 1: To this day,

VOICE 2: Tortoise,

VOICE 3: Rhinoceros,

VOICE 4: and Elephant

VOICE 5: are

TORTOISE, RHINO, ELEPHANT: best friends!

VOICES 1-5: Now we have a question for you. Who do you think is the greatest of the three?

Georgie Porgie

3 Readers: READERS 1,2; VOICE LEADER

READER 1: Hi, my name is_____. My name is not Georgie Porgie, but I am Reader One.

READER 2: Hi. My name is_____. My name is not Georgie Porgie, but I am Reader Two.

READER 1: This is a short poem.

VOICE LEADER:

About Georgie Porgie?

READER 2: Yes and

READER 1: about pudding and pie.

VOICE LEADER:

I like pudding

and I like pie.

READER 2: It is a poem of action,

READER 1: crying,

READER 2: playing,

READER 1: kissing

VOICE LEADER:

Not sure about this kissing stuff.

READER 2: and running.

VOICE LEADER:

I love Georgie!

Let's hear the poem!

Georgie Porgie

READER 2: Georgie Porgie,

READER 1: pudding and pie

READER 2: Kissed the girls

READER 1: and made them cry.

READER 2: When the boys

READER 1: came out to play,

ALL READERS: Georgie Porgie ran away.

VOICE LEADER:
There goooooooes Georgie,
running and kissing!

ALL READERS: Ole!

Goldilocks and the Three Bears

6 Readers: NARRATOR 1, 2; PAPA BEAR, MAMMA BEAR, BABY BEAR, GOLDILOCKS

NARRATOR 1: There were once three bears

NARRATOR 2: who had three gruff voices.

NARRATOR 1: The Papa Bear sounded like this—

PAPA BEAR: Loud gruff voice!

NARRATOR 2: Mamma Bear sounded like this—

MAMA BEAR: Soft gruff voice!

NARRATOR 1: And the little Baby Bear sounded like this—

BABY BEAR: Tiny gruff voice!

NARRATOR 2: When the three bears talked to one another they spoke in a—

PAPA BEAR: Loud gruff voice!

MAMA BEAR: Soft gruff voice!

BABY BEAR: Tiny gruff voice!

NARRATOR 1: Unlike other bears these three bears

NARRATOR 2: did not live in a cave.

NARRATOR 1: They lived in a house deep in the woods.

NARRATOR 2: And unlike other bears

NARRATOR 1: they all ate oatmeal in the morning.

NARRATOR 1,2: Hot oatmeal!

NARRATOR 2: But this particular morning

NARRATOR 1: the oatmeal was so hot it was too hot!

NARRATOR 2: After they had tasted the oatmeal

NARRATOR 1: they all agreed it was indeed

ALL BEARS: too hot!

NARRATOR 2: Papa Bear said in his loud gruffest voice,

PAPA BEAR: Let's go for a walk.

NARRATOR 1: The rest of the family agreed

NARRATOR 2: and said so in their own gruff voices—

MAMA BEAR: good idea.

BABY BEAR: good idea.

NARRATOR 1: And that is what they actually did.

NARRATOR 2: But, they forgot to lock the door,

NARRATOR 1: which is really understandable

NARRATOR 2: since most bear houses do not have doors

NARRATOR 1: and besides who comes to visits bears anyway?

NARRATOR 2: It wasn't long before Goldilocks,

NARRATOR 1: who was out jogging that morning,

NARRATOR 2: came upon the bears' house in the woods.

GOLDILOCKS: Hmm,

NARRATOR 1: said Goldilocks,

GOLDILOCKS: This must be a quaint cafe and motel.

NARRATOR 2: Since the door was open she went inside and called out,

GOLDILOCKS: Is anyone home?

NARRATOR 1: There was no answer.

GOLDILOCKS: This place must be a bed and breakfast inn.

NARRATOR 1: So, she made herself at home

NARRATOR 2: and sat down to eat breakfast.

GOLDILOCKS: This first big bowl of oatmeal is too salty!

NARRATOR 2: The second medium sized bowl of oatmeal was too sweet!

GOLDILOCKS: This third small bowl of oatmeal is just right!

NARRATOR 2: So, she promptly ate it all up.

NARRATOR 1: She was hungry enough to have eaten the other two bowls

NARRATOR 2: but they were just

GOLDILOCKS: too sweet and too salty!

NARRATOR 1: Beside the fireplace there were three chairs of three different sizes.

NARRATOR 2: As you might expect the large chair was Papa Bear's and it was

GOLDILOCKS: very hard, indeed!

NARRATOR 1: The middle sized chair was Mamma Bear's and it was

GOLDILOCKS: very soft. In fact, too soft.

NARRATOR 2: The small chair was Baby Bear's chair and it was

GOLDILOCKS: just right for sitting.

NARRATOR 1: Sitting may be for bears

NARRATOR 2: but not for the likes of Goldilocks;

NARRATOR 1: because even though she was a jogger

NARRATOR 2: she was just too heavy for the chair,

NARRATOR 1: and it broke in pieces!

NARRATOR 2: Goldilocks was heavier than Baby Bear!

GOLDILOCKS: They don't make things like they used to.

NARRATOR 1: Goldilocks picked herself up

NARRATOR 2: and went up the stairs to the bedrooms.

NARRATOR 1: And, as you might expect there were three beds.

NARRATOR 2: The first big bed was Papa Bear's bed and it was

GOLDILOCKS: very, very hard!

NARRATOR 2: The second medium sized bed was Mamma Bear's bed and it was

GOLDILOCKS: way too soft!

NARRATOR 2: The third smallest sized bed was Baby Bear's bed and it was

GOLDILOCKS: just right for sleeping.

NARRATOR 1: And sleep she did!

NARRATOR 2: After jogging and oatmeal

NARRATOR 1: Goldilocks needed a rest.

NARRATOR 2: In the meanwhile the bears, not knowing that Goldilocks

NARRATOR 1: had mistaken their house for a bed and breakfast,

NARRATOR 2: came home to eat their oatmeal.

NARRATOR 1: Once inside Baby Bear said

NARRATOR 2: in his tiny gruff voice,

BABY BEAR: Someone has eaten my oatmeal!

NARRATOR 1: The reason of course was that

GOLDILOCKS: it tasted just right!

NARRATOR 1: Papa Bear looked at his oatmeal and said in his loud gruff voice,

PAPA BEAR: No one ate mine,

NARRATOR 2: which was true because

GOLDILOCKS: it tasted too salty!

NARRATOR 1: Mamma Bear looked at her oatmeal and said in a soft gruff voice,

MAMA BEAR: No one ate mine either,

NARRATOR 2: which was true because

GOLDILOCKS: it tasted too sweet!

BABY BEAR: Look, look,

NARRATOR 1: said Baby Bear in his tiny gruff voice,

BABY BEAR: My chair is broken.

NARRATOR 2: The reason of course was because

GOLDILOCKS: his chair was just right!

NARRATOR 2: and she weighed more than Baby Bear.

PAPA BEAR: Look, look,

NARRATOR 2: said Papa Bear in his loud gruff voice,

PAPA BEAR: Someone has been sitting in my chair,

NARRATOR 1: which Goldilocks had sat in but found to be

GOLDILOCKS: very, very hard.

MAMA BEAR: Look, look,
NARRATOR 1: said Mamma Bear in her soft gruff voice,
MAMA BEAR: someone has been sitting in my chair,
NARRATOR 2: which Goldilocks had sat in but found to be
GOLDILOCKS: much, much too soft.
NARRATOR 1: When all at once they heard—snoring.
NARRATOR 2: So up the stairs they went.
NARRATOR 1: By now Papa Bear was very angry.
NARRATOR 2: Mamma Bear was very angry.
NARRATOR 1: Baby Bear was angry and sad.
PAPA BEAR: Look, look,
NARRATOR 2: said Papa Bear in his loud gruff voice,
PAPA BEAR: Someone has been in my bed.
MAMA BEAR: Look, look,
NARRATOR 1: said Mamma Bear in her soft gruff voice,
MAMA BEAR: Someone has been in my bed.
BABY BEAR: Look, look,
NARRATOR 2: said Baby Bear in his tiny gruff voice,
BABY BEAR: Someone has been in my bed.
NARRATOR 2: But he looked again and said,
BABY BEAR: Someone is in my bed!
ALL BEARS: Who are you? What do you want?
NARRATOR 1: Goldilocks immediately jumped out of the bed,
NARRATOR 2: ran down the stairs
NARRATOR 1: and out through the open door.
NARRATOR 2: Close behind her were the three bears
NARRATOR 1: trying to catch her and shouting in their gruffest voices,
ALL BEARS: Who are you? What do you want?
NARRATOR 1: But since Goldilocks had her breakfast of oatmeal and a good nap,
NARRATOR 2: she easily outran the bears.
NARRATOR 1: Here is one conclusion to this story.
NARRATOR 2: Jogging,
NARRATOR 1: depending on where you jog,
NARRATOR 2: may be dangerous to your health!

Homographic Pronunciation Fun

12 Readers: TEACHER, READERS 1-10, CLASS

TEACHER: What does L-E-A-D mean?
READER 1: Take charge.
TEACHER: Pronounce it.
CLASS: Lead.
READER 2: I think it means "the metal inside your pencil."
TEACHER: Pronounce it.
CLASS: Lead.

TEACHER: What does P-R-O-D-U-C-E mean?
READER 3: Make.
TEACHER: Pronounce it.
CLASS: Pro-duce´.
READER 4: I think it means "fruits and vegetables."
TEACHER: Pronounce it.
CLASS: Pro´-duce.

TEACHER: What does "D-E-S-E-R-T" mean?
READER 5: Dry, hot empty land.
TEACHER: Pronounce it.
CLASS: De´-sert.
READER 6: I think it means "abandon."
TEACHER: Pronounce it.
CLASS: De-sert´

TEACHER: What does "W-O-U-N-D" mean?
READER 7: Wrapped in a ball, like with string.
TEACHER: Pronounce it.
CLASS: Wound.
READER 8: I think it means "an injury."
TEACHER: Pronounce it.
CLASS: Wound.

TEACHER: What does "M-I-N-U-T-E" mean?
READER 9: Sixty seconds.
TEACHER: Pronounce it.
CLASS: Min´-ute
READER 10: I think it means "tiny."
TEACHER: Pronounce it.
CLASS: Min-ute´.

Homophonic Spelling Fun

16 Readers: TEACHER, READERS 1-15

TEACHER: What does "do" mean?
READER 1: Act.
TEACHER: Spell it.
CLASS: D-O.
READER 2: I think it means "morning moisture."
TEACHER: Spell it.
CLASS: D-E-W.
READER 3: I think it means "time to turn it in."
TEACHER: Spell it.
CLASS: D-U-E.

TEACHER: What does "rap" mean?
READER 4: Knock.
TEACHER: Spell it.
CLASS: R-A-P.
READER 5: I think it means "cover with paper."
TEACHER: Spell it.
CLASS: W-R-A-P.

TEACHER: What does "lesson" mean?
READER 6: Learning time.
TEACHER: Spell it.
CLASS: L-E-S-S-O-N.
READER 7: I think it means "get smaller."
TEACHER: Spell it.
CLASS: L-E-S-S-E-N.

TEACHER: What does "dessert" mean?
READER 8: After-dinner treat.
TEACHER: Spell it.
CLASS: D-E-S-S-E-R-T.
READER 9: I think it means "abandon."
TEACHER: Spell it.
CLASS: D-E-S-E-R-T.

TEACHER: What does "bite" mean?
READER 10: Gnaw out a piece.
TEACHER: Spell it.
CLASS: B-I-T-E.
READER 11: I think it means "a small computer unit."
TEACHER: Spell it.
CLASS: B-Y-T-E.

TEACHER: What does "brute" means?
READER 12: Big, mean guy.
TEACHER: Spell it.
CLASS: B-R-U-T-E
READER 13: I think it means "gossip."
TEACHER: Spell it.
CLASS: B-R-U-I-T

TEACHER: What does "carry-on" mean?
READER 14: Airplane luggage.
TEACHER: Spell it.
CLASS: C-A-R-R-Y-O-N.
READER 15: I think it means "vulture food."
TEACHER: Spell it.
CLASS: C-A-R-R-I-O-N.

House That Jack Built

5 Readers: READERS 1-4, AUDIENCE

ALL READERS: This is the house that Jack built.
READER 4: This is the malt,
ALL READERS: that lay in the house that Jack built.
READER 4: This is the rat,
READER 3: that ate the malt,
ALL READERS: that lay in the house that Jack built.
READER 4: This is the cat,
READER 2: that killed the rat,
READER 3: that ate the malt,
ALL READERS: that lay in the house that Jack built.
READER 4: This is the dog,
READER 1: that worried the cat,
READER 2: that killed the rat,
READER 3: that ate the malt,
ALL READERS: that lay in the house that Jack built.
READER 3: This is the cow with the crumpled horn,
READER 4: that tossed the dog,
READER 1: that worried the cat,
READER 2: that killed the rat,
READER 3: that ate the malt,
ALL READERS: that lay in the house that Jack built.
READER 2: This is the maiden all forlorn,
READER 3: that milked the cow with the crumpled horn,
READER 4: that tossed the dog,
READER 1: that worried the cat,
READER 2: that killed the rat,
READER 3: that ate the malt,
ALL READERS: that lay in the house that Jack built.
READER 4: This is the man all tattered and torn,
READER 1: that kissed the maiden all forlorn,
READER 2: that milked the cow with the crumpled horn,
READER 4: that tossed the dog,
READER 1: that worried the cat,
READER 2: that killed the rat,
READER 3: that ate the malt,

ALL READERS: that lay in the house that Jack built.
READER 4: This is the priest all shaven and shorn,
READER 3: that married the man all tattered and torn,
READER 1: that kissed the maiden all forlorn,
READER 2: that milked the cow with the crumpled horn,
READER 4: that tossed the dog,
READER 1: that worried the cat,
READER 2: that killed the rat,
READER 3: that ate the malt,
ALL READERS: that lay in the house that Jack built.
READER 4: This is the cock that crowed in the morn,
ALL READERS: Cock-doodle-do
READER 3: that waked the priest all shaven and shorn,
READER 4: that married the man all tattered and torn,
READER 1: that kissed the maiden all forlorn,
READER 2: that milked the cow with the crumpled horn,
READER 4: that tossed the dog, THAT TOSSED THE DOG,
READER 1: that worried the cat,
READER 2: that killed the rat,
READER 3: that ate the malt,
ALL READERS: that lay in the house that Jack built.
READER 4: This is the farmer sowing,
READER 2: that kept the cock that crowed in the morn,
ALL READERS: Cock-doodle-do.
READER 3: that waked the priest all shaven and shorn,
READER 4: that married the man all tattered and torn,
READER 1: that kissed the maiden all forlorn,
READER 2: that milked the cow with the crumpled horn,
READER 4: that tossed the dog, *that tossed the dog,* **that tossed the dog,**
READER 1: that worried the cat,
READER 2: that killed the rat,
READER 3: that ate the malt,
ALL READERS: that lay in the house that Jack built.
READER 4: Did Jack really build that house?
READER 2: No, I think it was actually Jill that built the house.
ALL READERS: The End.

Humpty Dumpty
3 Readers

READER 1: My last name is _____. I will read the part of Reader One.

READER 2: My last name is _____. I will read the part of Reader Two.

READER 3: My last name is _____. I will read the part of Reader Three.

READER 1: Humpty Dumpty

READER 3: may sound like

READER 1: a silly poem about eggs.

READER 2: It is a poem

READER 3: about walls and falls.

READER 1: It is a poem

READER 2: about horses and men.

READER 1: It is a poem

READER 3: about putting things

READER 2: together again.

READER 3: It is a poem

READER 1: that tells us to be careful where we go,

READER 2: how we sit,

READER 3: and what we do,

READER 2: and how we fall.

READER 1: Here is the poem called

READER 2: Humpty Dumpty!

READER 3: Humpty Dumpty

READER 2: sat on a wall,

READER 1: Humpty Dumpty

READER 2: had a great fall:

READER 3: All the King's horses

READER 1: and all the King's men can't put,

READER 3: can't put Humpty Dumpty together again.

READER 2: Poor Humpty Dumpty

READER 1: is all cracked up!

Into the Forest—A Prepositional Walk
4 GROUPS and 1 ACTOR called Charlie

GROUP 1: Charlie,

GROUP 4: Walked into the forest,*

GROUP 2: Jumped over a log,*

GROUP 3: Ducked under a branch.*

GROUP 1: Squeezed by some thorny bushes,*

GROUP 4: Stumbled across a patch of rocks,*

GROUP 2: Sloshed through a puddle,*

GROUP 3: Tiptoed behind a big tree,*

GROUP 4: Peeked around the trunk,*

GROUP 1: And put his hand to his mouth!*

GROUP 2: There it was,

ALL: The most beautiful deer in the whole wide world!

* After each line, actor Charlie mimes.

Jack

3 Readers: VOICE 1,2 and JACK

VOICE 1: Are you Jack?

JACK: Yes.

VOICE 2: I have heard so much about you.

JACK: Really.

VOICE 1: I haven't seen you for a long time.

JACK: Do you know me?

VOICE 2: Yes, I do.

JACK: When did we meet last?

VOICE 1: When you were in the box.

JACK: The Box?

VOICE 2: When did you get out?

JACK: Out of what?

VOICE 1: The Box, silly.

VOICE 2: You are Jack in the Box, are you not?

JACK: No, I am Jack who is quick.

VOICE 2: Can't believe it.

JACK: Believe what?

VOICE 2: How quick you must be to jump out of the box!

JACK: You've got the wrong Jack.

VOICE 1: Now I know who you are!

JACK: Really?

VOICE 1: You are the Cracker Jack!

JACK: The Cracker Jack?

VOICE 2: Yes, the Cracker Jack!

VOICE 1: The Jack who is quick and jumps.

JACK: I may be a cracker jack but I am not *the* Cracker Jack.

VOICE 1: Relative?

JACK: No, never heard of him. I am the Jack who is nimble.

VOICE 1: Tell me something.

JACK: Yes?

VOICE 2: If you are so nimble why did you fall down the hill?

JACK: I am the Jack who jumps, not falls.

VOICE 1: I suppose you don't know Jill then?

JACK: Never heard of her.

VOICE 1: You didn't go up the hill with Jill?

JACK: No, I didn't go up the hill with Jill.

VOICE 2: Wait a minute. Where do you get your water?

JACK: I don't get water up the hill and I don't get water with Jill.

VOICE 1: And how is your crown?

JACK: I am telling you that you have the wrong Jack.

VOICE 2: My apologies.

JACK: Apologies accepted.

VOICE 1: Now I know

VOICE 2: just who you are.

VOICE 1: You are the Jack that eats no fat.

JACK: Well, no.

VOICE 1: Then…

JACK: Actually I find a high-protein diet keeps me nimble and quick. I eat lots of meat.

VOICE 1: And apparently he doesn't mean lean meat.

VOICE 2: And he probably doesn't lick his plate either.

JACK: Furthermore, I do not have a wife.

VOICE 1: Ah, yes, you are the beanstalk Jack.

JACK: I am afraid of heights. Never jump any higher than 18 inches off the ground.

VOICE 2: You are the beanstalk Jack.

JACK: I am the candlestick Jack!

VOICE 2: Fee fie fo fum, Fee fie fo fum,

VOICE 1: Fee fie fo fum, I smell the blood of Jack.

JACK: Wrong Jack. I am the nimble Jack.

VOICE 2: Are you an Englishman?

JACK: I don't really know.

VOICE 1: You are nimble and quick?

JACK: Oh, yes, and I like to jump.

VOICE 2: Then you must be the beanstalk Jack

VOICE 1: to get away from the giant.

VOICE 2: Where is the goose?

JACK: The goose, the only *gooses* or geese around here are you two.

VOICE 1: Where is the golden egg?

JACK: You've got the wrong Jack!

VOICE 2: You say you are nimble?

JACK: Very much so.

VOICE 1: You say you are quick?

JACK: One of the quickest.
VOICE 2: You say that you jump?
JACK: Higher than a candlestick.
VOICE 1: Are the candles lit?
JACK: I think so.
VOICE 1: Are you afraid of fire?
JACK: Well, I don't like getting burned.
VOICE 1: Well, then I have it.
VOICE 2: I have it! I have it!
VOICE 1: I have a new poem about you, Jack!
JACK: Really?
VOICE 1: Jack, be nimble.
VOICE 2: Jack, be quick.
VOICE 1: Jack, jump over the candlestick.
JACK: It does have a nice ring to it.
VOICE 1: Jack, be nimble.
VOICE 2: Jack, be quick.
VOICE 1: Jack, jump over the candlestick.
JACK: Let's hear it again.
VOICE 1: Jack, be nimble.
VOICE 2: Jack, be quick.
VOICE 1: Jack, jump over the candlestick.
JACK: Publish it.

Multiple Meanings Fun

11 Readers: TEACHER, READERS 1-10, CLASS

TEACHER: What does "tire" mean?
READER 1: The wheel on a car.
READER 2: I think it means "get sleepy."
TEACHER: Spell it.
CLASS: T-I-R-E.

TEACHER: What does "fine" mean?
READER 1: OK.
READER 2: I think it means "a charge for breaking a rule."
TEACHER: Spell it.
CLASS: F-I-N-E.

TEACHER: What does "spoke" mean?
READER 1: Talked.
READER 2: I think it means "a radius on your bike wheel."
TEACHER: Spell it.
CLASS: S-P-O-K-E.

TEACHER: What does "post" mean?
READER 1: A pole sticking out of the ground.
READER 2: I think it means "mail."
TEACHER: Spell it.
CLASS: P-O-S-T.

TEACHER: What does "fret" mean?
READER 1: Worry.
READER 2: I think it means "a ridge on a guitar."
TEACHER: Spell it.
CLASS: F-R-E-T.

My First Friend

by Chip Gifford

3 Readers

READER 1: Excitement.

READER 2: Fear.

READER 3: Tension.

READER 1: Stress.

READER 3: Anticipation.

READER 2: Anxiety.

READER 1: Nerves.

READER 2: Sweaty palms.

READER 3: Dry mouth.

READER 1: Stomach noises.

READER 3: Alone.

READER 1: In a crowded room,

READER 2: looking,

READER 1: not seeing.

READER 2: Searching,

READER 3: but not finding.

READER 2: Finding only blank stares.

READER 1: Loud laughter.

READER 2: Quick,

READER 3: an awkward glance.

READER 2: Whispers.

READER 1: Muffled giggles.

READER 3: It seemed like eternity.

READER 2: Encapsulated

READER 1: in a half second

READER 2: of self-consciousness.

READER 1: With the question,

READER 3: the silent question,

READER 1: posed in the minds

READER 2: of countless

READER 3: school children.

READER 1: On the first day of school

READER 3: at lunch time,

READER 2: Who?

READER 1: Who can I sit with at lunch today?
READER 2: Scanning the tables,
READER 3: craning for a glimpse.
READER 1: Scouring dozens of faces.
READER 2: Fighting the urge
READER 1: to run,
READER 3: to run and never look back.
READER 2: But then
READER 1: eye contact.
READER 2: An inquisitive sparkle.
READER 3: (hard swallow, gulp sound effect)
READER 2: A grin
READER 3: breaks into a smile.
READER 2: A hand
READER 3: pats an empty place,
READER 1: pulls out the chair
READER 2: and gestures,
READER 3: sit here.
READER 1: In that eternal moment
READER 3: without a word,
READER 2: without formal introduction,
READER 3: without a conversation,
READER 3: I knew—
READER 1: within the silence,
READER 2: within this stranger,
READER 1: within this quiet,
READER 2: unspoken communication,
READER 1: I had found—
ALL: My first friend.

Radio Time

17 Readers: NARRATORS 1-4, GRANDPA, GRANDMA, DAD, MOM, SPORTSCASTER, BIOLOGIST, NEWSCASTER, INTERIOR DECORATOR, SCI-FI ACTOR, ENTERTAINMENT HOST, ENTERTAINMENT CELEBS HOST

NARRATOR 1: The Smiths were spending a long weekend at their cabin,
NARRATOR 2: but it was pouring rain, so they were stuck inside.
NARRATOR 3: They had played five rounds of Yahtzee, and now they were bored.
NARRATOR 1: Grandpa had an idea.
GRANDPA: Back when I was a boy, there was no TV, so we would sit around and listen to the radio. Shall we go retro?
GRANDMA, DAD, MOM, KEN, & KATHY: Ok, yeah, ok.

NARRATOR 2: The only difficulty was that all six of them had different interests.
NARRATOR 3: Each had his or her favorite station:
DAD: Sports Today
GRANDPA: The Biologist's Hour
GRANDPA: All News Station
MOM: Be an Interior Decorator
KEN: Sci-Fi Time
KATHY: Entertainment Celebs

NARRATOR 4: Listen to what happened as family members kept switching the stations.
SPORTSCASTER: As the NFL season nears its finish, it is clear that this has been an exceptionally good year for the Detroit…
BIOLOGIST: lions that have devoured many smaller animals. This provides a balance in nature, as these predators…
NEWSCASTER: pray for a safer world. These religious leaders have gathered to express their concern for those who are in need of…
Interior Decorator: more color in the kitchen. This area should be the brightest in…
SCI-FI ACTOR: the entire galaxy. Hang on tight. The enemy has just burst into the…
Kathy changes dial.

ADVERTISEMENT ANNOUNCER: Milky Way, the candy bar with that creamy, chocolaty taste that satisfies your hunger wherever you are. And now back to Entertainment Celebs.

ENTERTAINMENT CELEBS HOST: Our guest today is none other than Tom...

SCI-FI ACTOR: cruise through space with our lasers ready in case the enemy approaches the...

INTERIOR DECORATOR: bathroom, where candles give off a warm glow of light and the fragrance of...

BIOLOGIST: onions that attracts some animals but keeps others from approaching. Most animals have a strong sense of...

NEWSCASTER: obligation to the organizations that have poured millions of dollars into their campaign funds. This financial pressure is likely to increase legislators' interest in...

ENTERTAINMENT HOST: the romance between a city slicker and a country girl. As the tale unfolds, he proposes to her and gives her a...

SPORTS CASTER: pigskin. What a magical moment for the rookie kicker! We know he'll take the memento home and treasure it for the rest of...

SCI-FI ACTOR: the millennium. The time warp has changed our understanding of human development, as much as the lack of gravity has affected our ability to...

NEWSCASTER: stand up for what is right. The ethics committee must wrestle with yet another incident of politicians' using their positions to seek...

BIOLOGIST: grub worms as their main source of food. They root about in the soil and then feast on these slimy little critters by the hundreds on the...

INTERIOR DECORATOR: back patio, which provides a romantic setting for an evening picnic under the...

SPORTSCASTER: goal posts. The lions ate 'm alive today!

NEWSCASTER: And that is the news for this hour. Stay tuned for more...

SCI-FI: bizarre twists of life in outer space.

Sewing

6 Readers: VOICES 1-5, and AUDIENCE

VOICE 1: I wonder what happens when leaves get torn.
VOICE 2: Mother Nature mends them.
AUDIENCE: WHAT?!?
VOICE 2: Well, she has needles.
AUDIENCE: NEEDLES?!?
VOICE 1: Ah, you mean PINE needles.
VOICE 2: Yes, pine needles.
AUDIENCE: AH, pine needles.
VOICE 1: Hmm. It seems far-fetched to me, but tell me more.
VOICE 2: Help me with this rhyme.
AUDIENCE: OK.
VOICE 1: SEWING.
VOICE 2: If Mother Nature patches
VOICE 4: the leaves of trees and vines
VOICE 5: I'm sure she does her mending
AUDIENCE: with needles of pines!
VOICE 5: Yes, they are so long
VOICE 2: and slender,
VOICE 5: and somewhere in plain view,
VOICE 2: she has her threads of cobwebs
VOICE 3: and a thimble
AUDIENCE: full of dew?
VOICE 1: You have some imagination!
AUDIENCE: Yes, we DO!

Note: Select individuals or pairs for the Voice parts. The remaining students read the Audience lines.

Three Little Kittens

4 Readers: READER 1,2,3; VOICE LEADER

READER 1: One.

READER 2: Two.

READER 3: Three little kittens.

READER 2: Lost their mittens!

READER 1: And they began to cry,

ALL READERS: Oh, Mother dear,

VOICE LEADER: MEOW!

READER 2: we sadly fear our mittens,

ALL READERS: We have lost!

VOICE LEADER: What!

READER 3: We lost our mittens.

VOICE LEADER: You naughty kittens!

READER 1: Meow.

VOICE LEADER: Then you shall have no pie.

READER 2: Meow.

READER 3: Meow.

VOICE LEADER: MEOW!

READER 3: The one

READER 2: two

READER 1: three little kittens

READER 3: found their mittens,

READER 2: and they began to cry,

ALL READERS: Oh, Mother Dear,

READER 3: see here, see here.

READER 1: Our mittens we have found.

VOICE LEADER: What?

ALL READERS: We found our mittens.

VOICE LEADER: You good little kittens!

READER 2: What about our pie?

VOICE LEADER: Then you shall have some pie.

READER 1: Purr.

READER 2: Purr.

READER 3: Purr

VOICE LEADER: Purrrrrr.

READER 1: The end of purring and this story.

Three Little Pigs

7 Readers: NARRATOR 1, 2, 3; PIG 1, 2, 3; WOLF (AUDIENCE)

NARRATOR 1: Once upon a time there were three little pigs.

NARRATOR 2: And according to their mother

NARRATOR 3: it was time for them to leave home.

NARRATOR 2: It was time to leave the pigsty!

NARRATOR 1: In fact mother pig just told them to leave.

NARRATOR 3: After all

NARRATOR 1: there is only so much

NARRATOR 2: a pigsty can take.

NARRATOR 3: The three little pigs

NARRATOR 1: happily left home saying,

ALL PIGS: Goodbye, goodbye, goodbye.

NARRATOR 2: Or did they say,

ALL PIGS: Oink, oink, oink.

NARRATOR 3: Well whatever...

PIG 1: Let's work together or we just,

PIG 2: we just may be eaten—

AUDIENCE: by the Wolf!

NARRATOR 1: The pigs were wise in working together

NARRATOR 2: because the Wolf was—

AUDIENCE: very hungry!

NARRATOR 3: The three little pigs decided to build houses,

NARRATOR 2: instead of the usual pigsty.

NARRATOR 1: Pig Number One wanted a house.

PIG 1: I want it now.

NARRATOR 2: So he quickly built his house out of straw!

PIG 2: You are crazy!

PIG 3: The Wolf will

AUDIENCE: huff and puff

PIG 3: and blow your house down.

NARRATOR 2: But before the Wolf

AUDIENCE: huffed and puffed

NARRATOR 2: he knocked on the front door of the straw house.

AUDIENCE: Knock, knock, knock.

NARRATOR 2: and said,

AUDIENCE: Let me in.

ALL PIGS: Not by the hair of your chinny, chin, chin.
AUDIENCE: Let's have dinner together.
ALL PIGS: Not by the hair of your chinny, chin, chin.
NARRATOR 1: Which just made the Wolf very mad so, he
AUDIENCE: huffed and puffed
NARRATOR 1: and blew the house down.
NARRATOR 3: Pig Number One left out the back door
NARRATOR 2: just in time
NARRATOR 1: This made the Wolf very angry.
AUDIENCE: Growl, growl, growl.
NARRATOR 2: But he learned a valuable lesson.
NARRATOR 3: Pigs prefer to use the back door
NARRATOR 1: when there is trouble at the front.
NARRATOR 2: The Wolf was still
AUDIENCE: very hungry
NARRATOR 3: and thought he would visit—
NARRATOR 2: Pig Number Two.
NARRATOR 1: Pig Number Two had just finished building
PIG 2: a house out of sticks!
PIG 3: That is a crazy way to build a house.
NARRATOR 1: Which was true because the house had gaps and holes
NARRATOR 2: and could easily be blown over when the Wolf
AUDIENCE: huffed and puffed.
NARRATOR 3: When the Wolf did come
NARRATOR 1 to the house of sticks,
NARRATOR 2: he knocked on the <u>back</u> door.
NARRATOR 3: He had learned his lesson.
AUDIENCE: Knock, knock, knock.
NARRATOR 1: Then in his sweetest wolf voice said,
AUDIENCE: Let me in.
ALL PIGS: Not by the hair of your chinny, chin, chin.
AUDIENCE: Let's have dinner together.
ALL PIGS: Not by the hair of your chinny, chin, chin.
NARRATOR 2:Which made the Wolf very mad so he
AUDIENCE: huffed and puffed
NARRATOR 1: and blew the house down.
NARRATOR 3: Pig Number Two left
NARRATOR 2: out the front door just in time.

NARRATOR 3: This made the Wolf mad as hops.

AUDIENCE: Growl, growl, growl.

NARRATOR 2: But he learned a valuable lesson.

NARRATOR 1: You can't be in two places

NARRATOR 3: at the same time.

NARRATOR 2: The Wolf was still

AUDIENCE: very, very hungry.

NARRATOR 1: He was hungry enough to visit,

NARRATOR 3: Pig Number Three.

NARRATOR 2: By now the pigs had learned several things.

NARRATOR 1: If you build houses of straw and sticks

NARRATOR 3: sell them before the Wolf comes knocking

NARRATOR 2: and always use the right door.

PIG 3: Pig Number Three,

NARRATOR 1: who was the smartest pig ever,

NARRATOR 2: built his house out of bricks.

PIG 1: Good Idea.

PIG 2: Good Idea.

NARRATOR 2: The Wolf came to visit

NARRATOR 1: Pig Number Three.

NARRATOR 3: As was his custom

NARRATOR 2: he knocked on the door—

AUDIENCE: Knock, knock, knock.

NARRATOR 3: And said in a weak voice,

AUDIENCE: Let me in.

ALL PIGS: Not by the hair of your chinny, chin, chin.

AUDIENCE: Let's have dinner together.

ALL PIGS: Not by the hair of your chinny, chin, chin.

NARRATOR 2: Which of course made the Wolf very, very mad,

AUDIENCE: Growl, growl, growl. Mad, mad, mad.

NARRATOR 2: The Wolf in his anger shouted,

AUDIENCE: I will blow this house down.

NARRATOR 3: So he—

AUDIENCE: huffed and puffed

NARRATOR 3: and

AUDIENCE: huffed and puffed

NARRATOR 3: and

AUDIENCE: huffed and puffed

NARRATOR 3: while all the pigs chanted,
ALL PIGS: Not by the hair of your chinny, chin, chin.
Not by the hair of your chinny, chin, chin.
NARRATOR 1: The house of bricks stood firm!
NARRATOR 2: The Wolf, very much out of breath, sat down
NARRATOR 3: and scratched the hair
NARRATOR 2: on his chinny, chin, chin and said,
AUDIENCE: I am very hungry.
NARRATOR 1: And
AUDIENCE: I can outsmart these pigs.
NARRATOR 2: So he decided to wait on the roof,
AUDIENCE: where I can watch both doors.
When Pig Number Three comes out—
NARRATOR 3: Then,
AUDIENCE: then I will have a piggy back ride!
NARRATOR 2: While waiting on the roof
NARRATOR 3: he sat on the chimney's ledge
NARRATOR 2: lost his balance
NARRATOR 1: and fell down the chimney.
AUDIENCE: What a great way to get into the house!
NARRATOR 2: Awaiting him were the three little pigs
NARRATOR 3: and a big pot of boiling water.
NARRATOR 1: That night the three little pigs and the Wolf
NARRATOR 2: did have dinner together.
NARRATOR 3: Yes they did,
NARRATOR 1: they surely did and they had it
ALL PIGS: by the hair of his chinny, chin, chin!

The Three Wishes—An English Folktale

8 Readers: NARRATORS 1-4, ELF, WOODSMAN, WIFE, DOG

NARRATOR 1: Once upon a time

NARRATOR 2: There was a Woodsman

Woodsman puts broom handle on his shoulder.

NARRATOR 3: who went out to cut down a tree.

NARRATOR 1: He found a mighty oak and raised his ax.

NARRATOR 4: Suddenly a wee voice called out…

ELF: Stop! Do not cut this tree.

Woodsman lifts broom handle from shoulder and rests it on the floor.

NARRATOR 2: The Woodsman dropped his ax and…

All NARRATORs: Poof!

NARRATOR 3: Immediately, there stood before him a tiny ELF.

NARRATOR 4: The little fellow begged…

ELF: This tree is my home.

WOODSMAN: Your home?

ELF: Yes, my home. Please do not cut it down.

WOODSMAN: *Puts the broom handle back on his shoulder.*

But I am a Woodsman.

ELF: If you leave my tree alone then…

WOODSMAN: Then what?

ELF: *Holds up three fingers.*

Then I will grant you three wishes.

WOODSMAN: Any three wishes at all?

ELF: Any three wishes at all.

WOODSMAN: All right, but may I have time to think about my wishes?

ELF: Take your time. Just think of a wish and it will come true.

WOODSMAN: *Turns quarter left as though to leave.*

Thank you!

ELF: But remember.

WOODSMAN: *Turns back to original position.*

What?

ELF: *Assumes full back position and takes one step quarter right.*

You have only three wishes. Use them wisely.

Woodsman takes one step quarter left toward Wife and Dog.

NARRATOR 1: The Woodsman started home

NARRATOR 4: without any wood,

NARRATOR 3: but with great excitement.

NARRATOR 2: He could not wait to tell his Wife the good news.

NARRATOR 4: They could make such wonderful plans.

NARRATOR 1: He thought to himself,

WOODSMAN: I wish I were home right now!

All NARRATORs: Poof!

NARRATOR 3: Immediately, he was at home,

Wife and Dog face full front.

NARRATOR 2: sitting by the fire with his Wife.

WOODSMAN: *Lays the handle down.*

Oh, no!

NARRATOR 1: he cried.

NARRATOR 4: His Wife,

NARRATOR 3: looking startled,

NARRATOR 4: asked…

WIFE: What is the matter, dear?

NARRATOR 1: When the Woodsman told her what had happened,

NARRATOR 3: she said…

WIFE: It is all right, dear. I am glad you are home.

WOODSMAN: Yes, I am home.

WIFE: *Holds up two fingers.*

And you still have two wishes.

WOODSMAN: Yes, I do.

WIFE: You will just need to be more careful what you think.

WOODSMAN: Yes, I will.

NARRATOR 3: The Woodsman sat by the fire

NARRATOR 1: while his Wife began to make supper.

NARRATOR 2: He could smell his favorite sausage cooking in the kitchen.

NARRATOR 4: The fire was warm

Woodsman yawns.

NARRATOR 3: and he began to feel sleepy.

NARRATOR 2: So comfortable was he that didn't want to move.

Woodsman puts hand to mouth.

NARRATOR 1: He put his hand to his face

NARRATOR 2: to cover a contented yawn.

NARRATOR 3: He thought to himself…

WOODSMAN: I wish I had that sausage right here.

ALL NARRATORS: Poof!

NARRATOR 3: Immediately, a sausage flew

NARRATOR 2: right onto the Woodsman's

All NARRATORS: NOSE!

WOODSMAN: Oh, no!

NARRATOR 1: he cried.

NARRATOR 4: His Wife,

NARRATOR 3: looking startled,

NARRATOR 4: asked...

WIFE: What is the matter, dear?

NARRATOR 1: When the Woodsman told her what had happened,

NARRATOR 2: she said...

WIFE: It is all right, dear. I will pull the sausage from your nose.

NARRATOR 4: She pulled

NARRATOR 3: and he pulled.

NARRATOR 1: He pulled

NARRATOR 2: and she pulled.

NARRATOR 3: Even the dog came

NARRATOR 1: and pulled

NARRATOR 4: and they all pulled.

DOG: Woof!

NARRATOR 2: But the sausage would not leave the man's nose.

NARRATOR 1: Finally the Woodsman nodded sadly,

NARRATOR 3: and the Wife nodded sadly.

NARRATOR 4: Even the dog nodded sadly.

DOG: Woof, woof, woof!

NARRATOR 2: They all knew what he had to do.

NARRATOR 1: The Woodsman said aloud...

WOODSMAN: I wish this sausage were off my nose!

All NARRATORs: Poof!

NARRATOR 3: Immediately,

NARRATOR 1: the sausage fell from his nose.

NARRATOR 4: As they ate dinner,

NARRATOR 2: the Woodsman said...

WOODSMAN: I have never tasted better sausage.

WIFE: Thank you.

WOODSMAN: I wish I had never wanted more than the happiness I have had all along.

NARRATOR 3: The Woodsman nodded knowingly.

NARRATOR 2: His Wife nodded knowingly.
NARRATOR 4: Even the dog nodded knowingly.
Narrators step down from chairs and face full front. Elf faces full front.
DOG: Woof! Woof!
ALL READERS: The End.
All bow to the audience.

Presentational End Notes

- Aesop's "The Lion, the Wolf, and the Fox"—Since all students have parts, you will want to provide the entire class with copies of the script. This presentation is particularly effective when individual roles are assigned to all except the Wolf, whose lines are read chorally by the rest of the class members.

- Cinderella—Positioning of the readers is important. The narrators stand together on one side of the room or stage; the two stepsisters stand together on the other side; Cinderella sits on a chair off by herself. We have used this script, with its surprise twist at the end, as a model of a derivative tale. After a performance and analysis of this reading, students were asked to write their own versions of a common folk tale by "fracturing" one of the story elements (characters, setting, or plot line). We have found that this reading has great appeal for students in upper middle school, as well as high school.

- Friends, An Old African Tale—The effectiveness of this RT can be increased if the audience is divided into two groups assigned the lines of the elephant and the rhinoceros. The story line is played out with the elephant and rhinoceros (large number of readers) interacting with a tortoise (just one student). The role of the hare is not demanding and appears early in the presentation, making it ideal for a less proficient reader.

- Georgie Porgie—This reading requires the use of only three scripts, since the remainder of the class will be repeating after the voice leader.

- Goldilocks—During the first read-through, the teacher may want to read every other line, with the students chorally reading the alternate lines. This requires that the entire class attend to the text at all times. Next students can be divided into groups of six to prepare presentations for the class. If the class population is not divisible be six, pairs of readers can be assigned to the narrator parts, or, for that matter, any role. For a public presentation, individuals can be assigned to the character roles and the class divided into two groups to carry the narrator lines.

- Homographic Pronunciation Fun—Make two copies of the script, keeping one for yourself (teacher). Cut the other copy into segments, one per homograph pair. Distribute and assign individual roles.

(Example: Readers 1 and 2 have copies of lines 1-7 only.) Students then write their own lines using this starter as the pattern. When students note that there are two pronunciations and only one spelling, the differentiation between homophones and homographs become apparent.

- Homophonic Spelling Fun—Class members must listen carefully to the meaning clues in order to respond with the correct spellings. Again students should be encouraged to add their own lines.

- House That Jack Built—With some practice the readers can present an excellent reading for performance. A cadence is soon developed by the readers that makes the reading fun to preform and interesting to hear. The built-in repetition is particularly beneficial for second-language learners. See Chapter 7 for staging ideas.

- Humpty Dumpty—Since the reading requires only three readers, it is suggested that scripts be given to all and that every group of three practice and perform it for their classmates. Then, as reinforcement, Readers 1,2,3 can read chorally in a whole-class finale.

- Into the Forest—Students will need to practice the spoken lines first, while Charlie decides how to add his actions during a second reading. Because the students will want to look up after each line to watch Charlie, they will need to track print. What a good way to dispel the misperception that "following with the finger" is a "no-no." This script can be used over and over with different configurations. You could assign four readers and ask all other students to do the motions. Each day you could use four different readers. Repeating this short script in a variety of ways reinforces learning. Movement and repetition are especially appropriate for primary grades and second-language learners.

- Jack—Three readers need to practice these humorous lines to make the presentation come alive. As a follow-up activity, students could incorporate other "Jacks" into this RT.

- Multiple Meanings Fun—Use as for the Homographic and Homophonic scripts. Using the pattern, teams of students can create many additional lines. Students have genuine reasons to use the dictionary as they try to make longer and longer segments. The presentations are not as interesting as the homophones and homographs, but students do develop their context cluing skills, especially beneficial for English language learners.

- My First Friend—Students read this selection in groups of three and then discuss the various emotions expressed. The culmination is a full class discussion.

- Radio Time—The seven Radio Readers sit on stools in a semicircle facing the audience. The six family members, with backs to the audience, form a row facing the Radio Readers. Each of the six family members leans forward, as though changing the dial, just as his/her favorite station's line is to begin. Signs are hung on the readers, identifying their roles, to help the audience keep track during this rapid-fire exchange. See Chapter 7 for more detailed staging ideas.

- Sewing—This script calls for five Voices. These may be individuals or groups reading shared lines; but remember that Readers Theatre is a performance and students in general read better when there is an audience. A follow-up sorting activity can be used to reinforce understanding of the homophones included in the script.

- Three Little Kittens—This reading is best used as an entire-class activity.

- Three Little Pigs—This script calls for seven readers. The three pigs should be located five to ten feet apart. The main character, the Wolf, can move from pig to pig as he/she reads the wolf's lines. Or the audience can play the part of the wolf. Having the students make animal-like sounds as they read adds interest.

- Three Wishes—As with any RT practice increases the impact of the reading. Position the four narrators in a semi-circle about the other readers. Elevating the narrators on chairs so that they can look down on the elf, woodsman, wife and dog creates a stage in which the four later readers are the center of focus. See Chapter 7 for further staging ideas.

10

Science—Sample Scripts

In this chapter you will find a variety of scripts that we think would work well in the science classroom. While we wrote scripts with specific grade levels in mind we soon came to realize that the scripts could be used at a variety of grade levels. As a teacher you set the stage for whether a reading will be successful. Feel free to use these scripts either in the science area or in other classes to enhance student learning.

The alphabetical listing below gives an overview of the content and instructional focus of each script included in this chapter. At the end of the chapter is a matching alphabetical listing of scripts entitled **Presentational End Notes**. They contain our suggestions for ways these Readers Theatres could be used in the classroom.

- Bear, Bear, Bear—Introduces students to nature's ways of preserving life for its animals. This script was originally written for early elementary school children as the opening of a science lesson, but its repeated pattern also furthered their emergent reading skills.

- Biome Temperate Forest—Covers key information about the temperate forest biome. This script is especially effective as a review before an examination in a biology class. It could also be used to introduce the topic, as a check for prior knowledge or as the basis for discussion.

- Biome Tundra—Serves as a preview or a review for a unit on Biomes.

- Five Little Penguins—Introduces the fact that baby penguins do not enter the water until they have shed their baby down for scaly feathers. This script also gives students math practice in counting backward.

- How Do You Feel Today?—Stimulates discussion of mental health issues, an important part of the K-12 curriculum. Students can analyze this script to determine whether this therapy would be useful and/or to suggest other alternatives.

- Old Lady—Introduces the concept of food chains. After reading this fun, nonsense poem, students are ready to discuss real food chains found in nature.

- Raisin Fruit Relish—Introduces students to healthy ingredients in foods and can be used anywhere within a unit on foods and health. This humorous script is based on an actual recipe. As a follow-up, students can conduct analyses of food products, using nutritional values on store labels.

- Weather Wonderings: A Grain of Truth—Provides scientific explanations for old wives' tales about weather predictions.

- Zebra—Provides an anticipatory set for a lesson on animals that have strange colorations.

Bear, Bear, Bear

3 READERS: READER 1,2; AUDIENCE

READER 1: My name is_____.

READER 2: and my name is_____.

READER 1: We need your help

READER 2: to sing this song.

READER 1: Let's sing.

READER 2: Let's sing a song of

AUDIENCE: bear, bear, bear.

READER 1: He didn't have a thing,

READER 2: he didn't have a thing he could

AUDIENCE: wear, wear, wear.

READER 1: Sooooooooo

READER 2: he growled,

AUDIENCE: Grrrr,

READER 1: and scowled atrociously

READER 2: and grew himself

READER 1: a coat of

AUDIENCE: hair, hair, hair.

READER 1: And that is the poem

READER 1: about a bear who wore hair.

Biome Temperate Forest

6 Readers: TEACHER 1,2; STUDENT 1,2,3,4

STUDENT 1: We, the students,
STUDENT 2: will be asking
STUDENT 3: all the questions about the temperate biome.
STUDENT 4: You see for this biome,
ALL STUDENTS: we are in charge.
TEACHER 1: Yes, sirs
TEACHER 2: and madams!
TEACHER 1: In charge!
TEACHER 2: Indeed!
TEACHER 1: Ask on as if you know the questions
TEACHER 2: and the answers.
STUDENT 1: In the temperate forest
STUDENT 2: what kinds of animals are present?
TEACHER 1: Ah, bears.
ALL STUDENTS: No, no.
STUDENT 3: Black bears.
STUDENT 4: Please be more precise in your answer.
TEACHER 2: Sorry.
STUDENT 1: Name some more…
STUDENT 2: squirrels, beetles, deer, pumas, warthogs…
STUDENT 3: Stop!
STUDENT 4: Forget the pumas
STUDENT 2: and certainly forget the warthogs.
TEACHER 2: Just checking on you guys.
TEACHER 1: Warthogs and pumas are not in this biome.
STUDENT 3: What kinds of trees grow
STUDENT 4: in the temperate biome?
TEACHER 1: Deciduous trees.
TEACHER 2: That is to say, trees that lose
TEACHER 1: their leaves in the fall.
STUDENT 2: Be specific; name some.
TEACHER 2: Hickory,
STUDENT 4: a good wood for making baseball bats
STUDENT 3: and hickory sticks
STUDENT 2: to give whippings!

TEACHER 1: Maple trees,
STUDENT 4: the source of maple syrup
STUDENT 3: and beautiful furniture.
TEACHER 2: Beech and oak,
TEACHER 1: just to name a few.
ALL STUDENTS: Well done!
STUDENT 3: Where do you find such forests?
TEACHER 2: Don't you know?
STUDENT 1: We are asking the questions!
TEACHER 1: Yes, sir, and yes, madam.
TEACHER 2: Maine to Georgia,
TEACHER 1: Europe, China,
TEACHER 2: and Australia.
STUDENT 4: The temperature, is it hot or cold?
ALL TEACHERS: Both.
STUDENT 1: Explain, please.
TEACHER 2: It can be minus 24 to 110 degrees.
TEACHER 1: Furthermore it can rain.
STUDENT 2: How much?
TEACHER 2: Thirty to one hundred inches!
TEACHER 1: Usually gets lots of rain.
ALL STUDENTS: One more question.
STUDENT 1: Where do all the leaves go each fall?
BOTH TEACHERS: On the ground.
STUDENT 2: Don't get smart or else!
TEACHER 1: Honest, sirs and madams, we are only telling the truth.
TEACHER 2: The leaves fall to the ground each fall and rot all winter and spring.
TEACHER 1: The beetles and bugs love to live and eat in the rot.
TEACHER 2: Bears, that is black bears, love the beetles and insects,
TEACHER 1: as do the skunks.
TEACHER 2: Well, how did we do?
ALL STUDENTS: You skunked us all right!
TEACHER 1: Good. Now,
TEACHER 2: take out a piece of paper!

Biome Tundra

6 Readers: READER 1, 2; GROUP 1, 2, 3, 4

READER 1: I am the teacher
READER 2: of the great biome,
READER 1,2: The tundra.
GROUP 1: Who cares about the tundra?
GROUP 2: Yea, who cares about the tundra?
GROUP 3: Give us one good reason
GROUP 4: to learn about the TUNDRA.
READER 1: I will give you two good reasons.
ALL GROUPS: We have our biome ears on!! Ha, Ha.
READER 2: One,
READER 1: it is on the test!
ALL GROUPS: Oh!
READER 2: Two,
READER 1: if you don't pass this test
READER 2: you are going to live
READER 1: in the tundra,
READER 2: which is another name for
READER 1: Siberia!!
GROUP 2: Oh, great one,
GROUP 3: then teach us of the tundra.
READER 1: I thought you would see it my way.
READER 2: Pack you bags.
GROUP 4: Oh no, do we have to go?
READER 2: Pack your BAGS.
GROUP 2: OK, we will learn about the tundra.
READER 2: It will be just for a short visit.
ALL GROUPS: Let's go then!
READER 1: Good to see you so happy.
READER 2: Here is what
READER 1: you need to take.
READER 2: All your clothes
ALL GROUPS: Why?
GROUP 1: Remember you said,
GROUP 2: it was a short trip.
READER 1: Here is why you will have to keep warm.

READER 2: In the winter it may be
READER 1: minus 28 on the Celsius scale
READER 2: which is very cold.
GROUP 3: I want to stay here where it is warm.
GROUP 4: Stop whining!
READER 1: In the summer it may be
READER 2: 15 degrees above.
GROUP 1: In other words
ALL GROUPS: Leave the bathing suit at home.
GROUP 4: Sounds like a real
GROUP 1: drag of a place.
READER 1: While there you can
READER 2: ride a musk ox...
GROUP: Who is going to catch the musk ox?
READER 1: ...milk a caribou.
GROUP 3: No problem
READER 2: Have your picture taken
READER 1: with a penguin.
ALL GROUP: Smile everybody!
GROUP 3: I want my picture taken
GROUP 4: by a big tree.
READER 1: Sorry, no trees,
READER 2: only such things as
READER 1: mosses,
READER 2: and lichens,
READER 1: and grasses.
GROUP 1: While there
ALL GROUP: what are we going to eat?
READER 1: Grass with the caribou,
READER 2: blueberries with the musk ox,
READER 1: fish with the penguins.
GROUP 4: And what to drink?
GROUP 1: Try the milk from the caribou!!
GROUP: Yuk!
READER 2: One or two last things,
READER 1: maybe three or four last things.
READER 2: Bring boots for the winter,
READER 1: lots of snow,

READER 2: some rain,
READER 1: only about 15 centimeters
READER 2: of precipitation.
GROUP 1: Sounds like the desert to me.
GROUP 2: Sounds like Utah to me.
READER 1: The tundra has little precipitation.
GROUP 4: Which is another word for
ALL GROUPS: water.
GROUP 3: Is there any thing else?
READER 1: Yes.
READER 2: Yes.
READER 1: Don't forget the permafrost
READER 2: and the birds that nest there
READER 1: and that the land is flat.
GROUP 3: Hey, let's go to Alaska
GROUP 4: or Norway
GROUP 1: or Russia
ALL GROUPS: but not to the tundra.
READER 1: You will be surprised
READER 2: when you get there.
READER 1: All those places have tundras
READER 2: and Biology tests!!
ALL GROUPS: Oh, nooo…

Five Little Penguins—The Poem

Five little penguins waddle on the ice.
One falls in and says, "This doesn't feel nice."
Four little penguins waddle on the ice.
One falls in and says, "This doesn't feel nice."
Three little penguins waddle on the ice.
One falls in and says, "This doesn't feel nice."
Two little penguins waddle on the ice.
One falls in and says, "This doesn't feel nice."
One little penguin waddles on the ice.
He falls in and says, "This doesn't feel nice."
One mama penguin waddles on the ice.
She calls to her babies, "Hang on tight!"
She pulls and pulls and pulls and pulls and pulls till all five are out.
"Thank you, Mama!" the baby penguins shout.
Now six penguins feel, oh, so snug
As each baby penguin gives Mama a hug.

Five Little Penguins

6 Readers: TEACHER, PENGUINS 1-5

TEACHER: Five little penguins waddle on the ice.
One falls in and says,
PENGUIN 1: This doesn't feel nice.
TEACHER: Four little penguins waddle on the ice.
One falls in and says
PENGUIN 2: This doesn't feel nice."
TEACHER: Three little penguins waddle on the ice.
One falls in and says,
PENGUIN 3: This doesn't feel nice.
TEACHER: Two little penguins waddle on the ice.
One falls in and says
PENGUIN 4: This doesn't feel nice.
TEACHER: One little penguin waddles on the ice.

He falls in and says,
PENGUIN 5: This doesn't feel nice.
TEACHER: One mama penguin waddles on the ice.
She calls to her babies,
PENGUIN 6: Hang on tight!
TEACHER: She pulls* and pulls* and pulls* and pulls*
And pulls* till all five are out.
PENGUINS 1-5: Thank you, Mama!
TEACHER: the baby penguins shout.
Now six penguins feel, oh, so snug
As each baby penguin gives Mama a hug.
*On each "pull" Mama Penguin, bends over and picks up a baby using the scotch tape.

How Do You Feel Today?

Readers Theatre by Dusty Castro
4 Readers: NARRATORS 1,2, PSYCHOLOGIST, PATIENT (AUDIENCE)

NARRATOR 1: Life today is certainly not easy.
NARRATOR 2: Most of us
NARRATOR 1: could use more time
NARRATOR 2: to ourselves.
NARRATOR 1: to be free of the everyday
NARRATOR 2: stress and strain.
NARRATOR 1: Perhaps
NARRATOR 2: to be alone—
NARRATOR 1: lying on a deserted
NARRATOR 2: tropical island.
NARRATOR 1: But instead,
NARRATOR 2: some find themselves
NARRATOR 1: lying on office couches
NARRATOR 2: engaged in conversation
NARRATOR 1: with their only confidants.
NARRATOR 2: Talking.
NARRATOR 1: About what?
NARRATOR 2: Something like,
PSYCHOLOGIST: How do you feel today?
PATIENT: Disappointed.
PSYCHOLOGIST: Why is that?
PATIENT: No raise from the boss.
PSYCHOLOGIST: You expected it soon?
PATIENT: He said this week.
PSYCHOLOGIST: That is quite a disappointment.
PATIENT: A big one.
PSYCHOLOGIST: Other feelings?
PATIENT: Definitely perplexed.
PSYCHOLOGIST: Over what?
PATIENT: I don't understand the ways of the world.
PSYCHOLOGIST: Read the news, do you?
PATIENT: Too much I suppose.
PSYCHOLOGIST: Anything else?
PATIENT: Well, a bit helpless.

PSYCHOLOGIST: How so?

PATIENT: Had my third flat tire yesterday, over the last month!

PSYCHOLOGIST: And you can't change one, right?

PATIENT: Pretty bad, huh?

PSYCHOLOGIST: You feel helpless, but it's not at all hopeless.

PATIENT: That's good to hear.

PSYCHOLOGIST: Is that all you're feeling?

PATIENT: Just one last thing, I'm anxious.

PSYCHOLOGIST: For what?

PATIENT: My four tickets.

PSYCHOLOGIST: The cops got you that bad?

PATIENT: No, the lottery's got me hooked.

PSYCHOLOGIST: The money's big now?

PATIENT: Sure is.

PSYCHOLOGIST: Well, you can't win 'em all!

NARRATOR 1: Is that the end?

NARRATOR 2: That's just one session.

NARRATOR 1: Does it ever get better?

NARRATOR 2: Listen to the rest.

PSYCHOLOGIST: Feeling better today?

PATIENT: Much relieved.

PSYCHOLOGIST: What an improvement!

PATIENT: Yeh. My luck. I won.

PSYCHOLOGIST: The big money?

PATIENT: Biiiig money!

PSYCHOLOGIST: So we're through.

PATIENT: Seems so.

PSYCHOLOGIST: Perhaps so.

NARRATOR 1: NOT SO!

NARRATOR 2: Is that so?

NARRATOR 1: He'll be back.

Old Lady

5 Readers: READERS 1,2,3,4; AUDIENCE

READER 1: There was an old lady who swallowed a fly.

READER 2: I don't know why she swallowed a fly.

AUDIENCE: Perhaps she'll die.

READER 1: There was an old lady who swallowed a spider

READER 3: that wriggled and wriggled and jiggled inside her.

READER 4: She swallowed the spider to catch the fly.

READER 2: I don't know why she swallowed a fly.

AUDIENCE: Perhaps she'll die.

READER 1: There was an old lady who swallowed a bird.

READER 4: She swallowed the bird to catch the spider,

READER 3: that wriggled and wriggled and jiggled inside her.

READER 4: She swallowed the spider to catch the fly.

READER 2: I don't know why she swallowed a fly.

AUDIENCE: Perhaps she'll die.

READER 1: There was an old lady who swallowed a cat.

READER 3: Well, fancy that, she swallowed a cat!

READER 2: She swallowed the cat to catch the bird.

READER 4: She swallowed the bird to catch the spider,

READER 3: that wriggled and wriggled and jiggled inside her.

READER 4: She swallowed the spider to catch the fly.

READER 2: I don't know why she swallowed a fly.

AUDIENCE: Perhaps she'll die.

READER 1: There was an old lady who swallowed a dog.

READER 2: What a hog, to swallow a dog!

READER 1: She swallowed the dog to catch the cat.

READER 2: She swallowed the cat to catch the bird.

READER 4: She swallowed the bird to catch the spider,

READER 3: that wriggled and wriggled and jiggled inside her.

READER 4: She swallowed the spider to catch the fly.

READER 2: I don't know why she swallowed a fly.

AUDIENCE: Perhaps she'll die.

READER 1: There was an old lady who swallowed a cow.

READER 2: I don't know how she swallowed a cow!

READER 3: She swallowed the cow to catch the dog.

READER 1: She swallowed the dog to catch the cat.

READER 2: She swallowed the cat to catch the bird.
READER 4: She swallowed the bird to catch the spider,
READER 3: that wriggled and wriggled and jiggled inside her.
READER 4: She swallowed the spider to catch the fly.
READER 2: I don't know why she swallowed a fly.
AUDIENCE: Perhaps she'll die.
READER 1: There was an old lady who swallowed a horse.
AUDIENCE: Perhaps she'll die.
READER 4: Perhaps? Perhaps?
ALL READERS: She's dead!
READER 1: Of course.

Raisin Fruit Relish

6 READERS: COOKS 1,2,3,4; GUESTS 1,2

COOK 1: A gift from your kitchen

COOK 2: is a gift from the heart.

GUEST 1: I like gifts from the kitchen.

GUEST 2: This is a different gift.

COOK 3: It is called

COOK 4: Raisin Fruit Relish.

GUEST 1: That is a strange name!

GUEST 2: I wonder what it tastes like.

COOK 1: It is a confetti combination of raisins,

COOK 2: of fresh fruit.

GUEST 1: So far so good.

COOK 4: of red and green bell peppers.

GUEST 2: I am having my doubts!

GUEST 1: Is that the gift?

COOK 3: It takes only ten minutes to make.

GUEST 1: But

GUEST 2: what will it taste like?

COOK 2: It's sweet

COOK 3: and tangy

COOK 1: a real delight.

GUEST 1: Let me decide, OK?

COOK 1: It tastes good with meats

COOK 2: and treats

COOK 3: and most anything you eat.

GUEST 1: All this is a gift?

GUEST 2: Some gift!

GUEST 1: Maybe it tastes better than it sounds.

COOK 4: Get your pencils out

COOK 3: for this yummy recipe.

GUEST 2: Yummy?

COOK 3: Two cups vinegar.

GUEST 1: Ouu…sounds sour!

COOK 4: Two cups sugar.

GUEST 2: Ahh…sounds better.

COOK 3: Four cups apples.

GUEST 1: Hmmm…I like apples!
COOK 1: One cup red bell peppers.
COOK 2: Four cups raisins.
COOK 3: One-third cup ginger.
GUEST 1: What do you do with the vinegar and raisins and ginger
GUEST 2: and red peppers and apples and bell peppers?
COOK 4: Listen up now.
COOK 3: Mix,
COOK 2: add, simmer, mix some more.
COOK 4: Then—Boil,
COOK 1: simmer again, cool, drain, store, serve.
COOK 2: Now just—Eat,
COOK 3: and eat, eat, and eat.
COOK 4: It makes 8cups!
GUEST 1: So—let's all eat.
GUEST 2: Hmmm…
GUEST 1: We'll take some more!
GUEST 2: Let's see—is there any left over?
COOK 2: Are you kidding?
ALL READERS: Plllenty.

Weather Wonderings: Grain of Truth

24 Readers: VOICES 1-24

ALL: A Grain of Truth
VOICE 1: If you have ever lived in a farm community,
VOICE 2: you know that there are silly little sayings
VOICE 3: about ways you can tell when the weather will
VOICES 1-3: change.
VOICE 1: But are they just wives' tales, or—
VOICE 2: do they contain
VOICES 1-3: a grain of truth?

ALL: When sheep gather in huddles,
 Tomorrow we'll have puddles.
VOICE 4: A sheep's wool traps air as insulation,
VOICE 5: so when the air turns cold,
VOICE 6: sheep feel chilly.
VOICE 4: To keep warm,
VOICES 4-6: they move close together.

ALL: When clouds look like black smoke.
 A wise man puts on his cloak.
VOICE 7: Meteorologists know that several cloud patterns usually produce
VOICES 7-9: rain or snow.
VOICE 8: Flat,
VOICE 9: gray,
VOICE 7: altostratus clouds,
VOICE 8: which form in layers,
VOICE 9: may cause
VOICES 7-9: rain or snow.
VOICE 7: When altostratus clouds thicken
VOICE 8: and drift low,
VOICE 9: they form dark,
VOICE 7: ragged
VOICE 8: nimbostratus clouds
VOICE 9: from which continuous rain or snow falls.

VOICE 7: Cumulonimbus clouds may build into towering formations that bring
VOICES 7-9:THUNDERSTORMS.

ALL: When the cow scratches her ear,
    It means a shower is near,
    But when she thumps her ribs with her tail
    Expect thunder, lightning and hail.
VOICE 10: Low atmospheric pressure
VOICE 11: and increased humidity
VOICE 12: cause the hairs inside a cow's ear to
VOICES 10-12: wiggle.
VOICE 10: This may tickle
VOICE 11: and make her scratch.
VOICE 12: Before a violent storm,
VOICE 10: static charges may make a cow's hair
VOICES 10-12: stand straight up.
VOICE 11: To try to relieve the discomfort this causes,
VOICE 12: she may brush herself with her tail
VOICES 10-12: over and over again.

VOICES 1-3: The owls hoot,
VOICES 4-6: the peacocks toot,
VOICES 7-9: the ducks quack,
VOICES 10-12: frogs yak—
ALL: 'twill rain.
VOICES 13-15: The loons call,
VOICES 16-17: swallows fall,
VOICES 19-21: chickens hover,
VOICES 22-24: groundhogs take cover—
ALL: 'twill rain.

VOICE 13: Cows are not the only creatures who sense coming rain.
VOICE 14: Many animals respond to the low pressure
VOICE 15: and high humidity
VOICES 13-15: just before a storm.
VOICE 13: They become uncomfortable,

VOICE 14: restless, and
VOICES 13-15: NOISY.

ALL: A circle around the moon
     'Twill rain soon.
VOICE 16: The high,
VOICE 17: feathery clouds
VOICE 1: called cirrostratus clouds
VOICE 16: are made entirely of
VOICES 16-17: ice crystals.
VOICE 17: The ice crystals refract light
VOICE 16: and create haloes around the moon.
VOICE 17: These clouds do not directly cause precipitation,
VOICES 17-18: but they frequently become water-heavy at lower altitudes,
VOICE 16: and soon comes a
VOICES 16-18: STORM.

VOICES 1-12: Rainbow in the morning,
VOICES 13-24: shepherds take warning.
VOICES 1-12: Rainbow at night
VOICES 13-24: shepherds' delight.

VOICE 19: When rain clouds
VOICE 20: filled with moisture
VOICE 21: are in the west
VOICE 19: and the morning sun shines on them
VOICE 20: from the east,
VOICES 19-21: a rainbow forms.
VOICE 21: The water droplets scatter the sun's rays
VOICE 19: and the colors of the spectrum appear.
VOICE 20: Many storms move west
VOICE 21: to east,
VOICE 19: so a morning rainbow in the east
VOICE 20: usually comes before a rain.
VOICE 21: If the setting sun shines on clouds in the east,
VOICE 19: it means that the clouds have already passed by
VOICES 19-21: and the rain is over.

VOICE 22: Are weather jingles
VOICE 23: just wives' tales,
VOICE 24: or do they, in fact, contain
ALL: a grain of truth?

The Zebra

5 Readers

ALL READERS: The zebra, the zebra, the zebra
READER 1: has such a funny hide.
ALL READERS: The zebra, the zebra, the zebra—
READER 3: We never can decide
READER 4: whether he's white
READER 2: with stripes of black,
READER 3: or black
READER 2: with stripes of white.
ALL READERS: Oh, zebra,
READER 5: oh, zebra, oh, zebra,
READER 3: Oh, tell us which is right—
READER 4: White stripes on black
ALL READERS: Or black stripes on white?

Presentational End Notes

- Bear, Bear, Bear—The teacher and another reader (possibly a student) read the Reader 1 and 2 lines. The script is projected on a screen so the students can follow along with one of the Readers pointing to the lines they are to read (say). For repeated readings students may be assigned the readers' lines.

- Biome Temperate Forest—Asking six students to practice the day before presentation ensures a more polished reading; everyone is then able to focus on the content rather than the mechanics of the presentation.

- Biome Tundra—Divide the audience into four groups. Two students take the readers' lines. If needed the teacher can read the lines of both Readers 1 and 2.

- Five Little Penguins—The teacher presents the poem first to the entire class. (This allows for the possibility of using full-class choral reading of the teacher lines on repeated readings.) Make five small and one large finger puppet. Put 5 strips of clear scotch tape on the Mama penguin. Place a table in front of the presenters. Assign penguin roles and show Penguins 1-5 how to drop the puppets as though into the water. If you choose to have an advanced student read the teacher lines (Mama Penguin), show him/her how to pick up the 5 babies using the scotch tape strips.

- How Do You Feel Today?—Casting the Audience as the Patient is a very effective way to engage the entire class.

- Old Lady—Dividing the class into groups of four, with all four reading the Audience lines, makes this RT a sure hit with the students. The teacher circulates among the groups giving suggestions for acting with their voices. (They will not need much prompting!). For a final reading, you might choose four solo readers and a cue-card holder to prompt the Audience lines by the remainder of the class.

- Raisin Fruit Relish—As an option to assigning an individual to read each part, four students may be assigned to the Cook roles. The remaining students are divided into two groups to read the Guest 1 and

Guest 2 lines. To add interest, one teacher actually prepared the Relish and had the students at least taste it!

- Weather Wonderings: A Grain of Truth—This script is based on six poetic sayings and can be presented as shared in this chapter. Alternatively, if you have students ready to learn to create their own scripts, the unaltered text (i.e., not formatted as a RT script) can be given to the class and used for a full-class and/or small group script-writing activity. The version included here was, in fact, prepared by students during a weather study. See Chapter 6 for further instructional suggestions.

- Zebra—The teacher alternates lines with the students. This helps children read their lines with ease. Then the students are divided into groups of four to read the script among them. As a follow-up, the students can write short RTs about other different-looking animals, hence integrating science and language arts.

11

Mathematics—Sample Scripts

We have found that elementary and high school students enjoy reading scripts dealing with mathematics. Usually they are pleasantly surprised when a teacher involves them in such a non-traditional activity.

This chapter contains scripts that illustrate what can be done in mathematics with the spoken word. We invite you to use them and to prepare your own as instructional tools that enhance mathematics learning while fostering your students' literacy development.

The alphabetical listing below gives an overview of the content and instructional focus of each script included in this chapter. At the end of the chapter is a matching alphabetical listing of scripts entitled **Presentational End Notes**. They contain our suggestions for ways these Readers Theatres could be used in the classroom

- Angles—Explains the three basic types of angles and helps students visualize the endless widening of angles until a circle is formed.

- Balloons—Gives practice in regrouping for subtraction in a word problem approach.

- Country Man City Man—Provides students with a layman's perspective on technology with a humorous ending.

- How Big is PI—Introduces, reinforces, and/or reviews concepts related to the area of a circle. This script is fun to read and listen to, and always conjures up smiles on the faces of students.

- Negative-Positive Tug of War—Introduces the concept of negative and positive numbers.

- One Two Buckle My Shoe—Gives students practice in counting and reading number words.

- Shapes—Provides an interesting way to check students' prior knowledge at the beginning of a unit on plane geometric figures, and then their acquired knowledge of these terms after instruction.

- Twinkle Twos—Demonstrates the function of "0" in place value, while giving students practice in counting by twos.

- Vocal Parabola—Helps students understand what a parabola is, by having them make one with their voices.

Angles
5 Readers: READERS 1-4; ANGLE

READER 1: Let me tell you a story

READER 2: and I am here to tell you

READER 3: it is a true story!

READER 2: It is how Sally Straight became Angie Acute and

READER 4: became Trisha Triangle,

READER 3: then Ruth Rectangle,

READER 4: then Patty Pentagon,

READER 2: then Helen Hexagon,

READER 1: then Olivia Octagon,

READER 3: and finally Cecilia Circle.

READER 4: To begin with her name was Sally Straight.

ANGLE: I have decided to go straight!

READER 1: When asked what her angle was she simply stated,

ANGLE: One hundred eighty degrees, no more no less.

READER 3: As you might expect a straight line is not very exciting.

READER 4: So she changed her name to Angie Acute

READER 2: and I am here to tell you that she was acute,

READER 4: sharp,

READER 1: to the point,

READER 2: and like a wedge.

ANGLE: I am less than ninety degrees but more than zero degrees.

READER 3: One day in an effort to find herself a place in life

READER 4: she tried the circle.

ANGLE: I have no use for circles!

READER 2: Really.

ANGLE: I just don't fit into a circle.

READER 1: Yet there were circles all about her:

READER 2: Car tires,

READER 3: The sun,

READER 4: The moon (when it was full),

READER 2: Circles under people's eyes,

READER 3: Donuts,

READER 4: Hula hoops,

READER 1: CD's

READER 2: And on and on.

ALL READERS: Soooooooooo
READER 3: She got together with two other angles
READER 4: and formed,
READER 2: you may have guessed it—
ANGLE: a triangle. Call me Trisha Triangle.
READER 1: She liked that because in the triangle
ANGLE: the other two angles insisted that I stay acute.
READER 2: So she was a part of
READER 3: pizza slices,
READER 4: pieces of pie,
READER 2: sides of pyramids,
READER 3: musical triangle and
READER 1: and, and, I can't think of any more.
READER 4: Moving right along.
READER 3: That was when she was young.
READER 1: As she grew larger—
ANGLE: I have become just right
READER 4: and admired by all sorts of people.
READER 3: Everyone called her Right Angle.
READER 2: Asked what angle she was working now, she would say,
ANGLE: Ninety degrees, no more no less.
READER 1: Others would ask about her looks
READER 4: and people would say she was All Right.
READER 3: Right Angle, being a party animal, joined up with three other right angles
READER 2: and they became a rectangle.
ANGLE: I am now to be known as Ruth Rectangle.
READER 1: They were a rather rigid group but they served good purposes:
READER 4: Buildings,
READER 2: Boxes,
READER 3: Floor tiles,
READER 2: Windows,
READER 3: Duplicating paper,
READER 2: Envelops,
READER 3: Eassette holders,
READER 1: Picture frames,
READER 4: and on and on.
READER 1: Right Angle seemed to never be satisfied

READER 2: and so she grew, and no longer was just Right.

ANGLE: I have become obtuse.

READER 4: Just what does that mean?

ANGLE: I am between just Right and Straight.

READER 3: Give us some degrees if you please.

ANGLE: Greater that ninety and less than one hundred eighty, no more, no less.

READER 1: What is next?

ANGLE: I have big plans.

READER 1: She looked about and joined four other obtuse angles.

READER 4: Together they become a pentagon.

ANGLE: Call me Patty Pentagon.

READER 3: The five added another obtuse angle

READER 2: And they named themselves hexagon.

ANGLE: I like the name Helen Hexagon.

READER 4: They added two more obtuse angles

READER 2: and they became an octagon.

ANGLE: I don't really care for the name Olivia Octagon.

READER 1: Wait, is there no stopping the obtuse angles from joining with more and more obtuse angles?

READER 4: No, I don't think so.

READER 2: They kept adding and adding obtuse angles

READER 3: until one day she looked at herself in a mirror

READER 1: and with horror screamed,

ANGLE: I have become a circle. Help! Help!

READER 3: But it was too late.

READER 3: People from henceforth called her Cecilia Circle,

READER 4: a name she really hated.

READER 1: The Angie Acute had become too obtuse for her own good.

READER 2: The moral of the story is this:

READER 1: Be careful who and how many you run with

READER 3: because you may end up

ALL READERS: running around in circles.

Balloons

11 Readers: TEACHER, STUDENTS 1-10

ALL: It's carnival time!

STUDENT 1: We need to put out the balloons.

TEACHER: Here they are, 10 boxes with 10 in each box.

STUDENT 1: Thanks. Hey, guys. Come get the balloons for your booths.

STUDENT 2: Dunking Booth. I need 9. Thanks.

STUDENT 3: Fish Net Booth. I need 7. Hey, there's only 1* here.

STUDENT 1: Well, crack open another box to get the rest.

STUDENT 3: OK. Thanks.

STUDENT 4: Roller Ride. I need 8. Hey, there are only 4 * here.

STUDENT 1: Well, crack open another box to get the rest.

STUDENT 4: OK. Thanks.

STUDENT 5: Go Carts. I need 9. Hey, there are only 6 * here.

STUDENT 1: Well, crack open another box to get the rest.

STUDENT 5: OK. Thanks.

STUDENT 6: Pitch a Ball. I need 8. Hey, there are only 7 * here.

STUDENT 1: Well, crack open another box to get the rest.

STUDENT 6: OK. Thanks.

STUDENT 7: Ring the Bear. I need 9. Hey, I got just what I need! Thanks!

STUDENT 8: Cake walk. I need 7. Hey, the box is empty.

STUDENT 1: Well, crack open another box.

STUDENT 8: OK. Thanks.

STUDENT 9: Hook the Crook. I need 6. Hey there are only 3 * here.

STUDENT 1: Well, crack open another box to get the rest.

STUDENT 9: OK. Thanks.

STUDENT 10: Dunk the Teacher. All the kids will come to my booth. Give me everything you've got left.

STUDENT 1: OK. But I have to keep a record of how many you took. Count them out and you may have them.

STUDENT 10: Never mind. The kids will come anyway.

*These numerals may be whited out of the script and supplied by the students upon solving the subtraction problems.

Country Man City Man

6 Readers: READERS 1-4; CITY MAN, COUNTRY MAN

READER 1: A shepherd was herding his flock in a remote pasture

READER 2: when suddenly a brand-new BMW

READER 3: advanced out of the dust cloud towards him.

READER 4: The driver,

READER 2: a young man in a 100 % silk suit,

READER 3: Italian shoes,

READER 4: mod sunglasses,

READER 1: and a very expensive necktie

READER 3: leaned out the window and asked the shepherd,

CITY MAN: If I tell you exactly how many sheep you have in your flock, will you give me one?

READER 1: The shepherd looked at the man,

READER 2: obviously a urbane yuppie,

READER 3: then looked at his peacefully grazing flock and calmly answered,

COUNTRY MAN: Sure.

READER 3: The yuppie parked his car,

READER 4: whipped out his notebook

READER 1: and connected it to a cell phone.

READER 2: Then he surfed to a NASA page on the Internet

READER 3: where he called up surveillance satellite system,

READER 4: scanned the area,

READER 3: opened up a database,

READER 2: and an Excel spreadsheet with complex formulas.

READER 1: He sent an email on his wireless cell phone

READER 4: and, after a few minutes, received a response.

READER 2: Finally,

READER 1: he prints out a 150 page report on his hi-tech, miniaturized printer,

READER 2: then turns to the shepherd and says,

CITY MAN: You have exactly 1586 sheep.

COUNTRY MAN: That is correct; take one of the sheep.

READER 2: The shepherd watches the young man select one of the animals

READER 4: and bundles it into his car.

READER 1: Then the shepherd says:

COUNTRY MAN: If I can tell you what your business is, will you give me back my sheep?
CITY MAN: OK, why not.
COUNTRY MAN: Clearly, you are a consultant.
CITY MAN: That's correct but how did you guess that?"
COUNTRY MAN: No guessing required.
CITY MAN: Really!
COUNTRY MAN: You turned up here although nobody called you.
CITY MAN: Well.
COUNTRY MAN: You want to get paid for an answer I already knew...
CITY MAN: But, I thought—
COUNTRY MAN: ...to a question I never asked and you don't know anything about my business. Now give me back my dog.

How Big is That Pi?

by Randy Nomura

2 Readers

READER 1: The area of a circle is pi r squared.

READER 2: Pie are squared?

READER 1: Yes, pi r squared!

READER 2: But, I thought pies are round?

READER 1: Pies are round!

READER 2: But you said pie are squared!

READER 1: Not pie are squared! Pi r squared!

READER 2: Pie are squared?

READER 1: Yes. the area of a circle is pi r squared!

READER 2: Wouldn't it be more proper to say pie is squared?

READER 1: Pi is squared?

READER 2: Yes, pie is singular therefore pie is squared!

READER 1: Pi r squared is a formula. What about the r?

READER 2: Are what?

READER 1: Not 'are' what! The 'r' is for radius!

READER 2: The radius are what?

READER 1: The radius is what!

READER 2: The radius is what?

READER 1: The radius is the line segment that joins the center of the circle to a point on the circle!

READER 2: Huh?

READER 1: The radius is also one half of the diameter!

READER 2: Huh?

READER 1: Diameter!

READER 2: Diameter?

READER 1: Distance across the circle. Diameter!

READER 2: Is that equal to two meters?

READER 1: Two meters?

READER 2: Yes, two meters! Doesn't 'di' mean two?

READER 1: Well, I guess it would if the circle was big enough!

READER 2: What circle?

READER 1: The two-meter circle.

READER 2: A two-meter circle is called a diameter?

READER 1: No, the diameter is twice the radius!

READER 2: So, the radius is equal to a meter!

READER 1: No, the radius is the distance from the middle of the pie to the crust!

READER 2: So how you measure the distance of the pie?

READER 1: Pi is approximately 3.14.

READER 2: The pie is 3.14 what!

READER 1: Whatever units you are using!

READER 2: My units are pies!

READER 1: Not are pies! Pi r squared!

READER 2: I get it!!! The pies that are squared are two meters across and have a round crust like the middle area of approximately 3.14 circles! I'm so smart!

READER 1: I'm hungry!

Negative-Positive Tug of War

7 Readers: STUDENTS 1-4, KARL, BEN, MIKE

STUDENT 1: Karl is so negative!

STUDENT 2: He never has anything good to say about anything

STUDENT 3: or anyone.

STUDENT 1: And his buddy, Ben! Sheesh!

STUDENT 4: He just adds fuel to the fire.

STUDENT 3: Yeh, things get even "negativer!"

STUDENT 1: to coin a word.

STUDENT 4: His cousin—what's his name?

STUDENT 2: Mike?

STUDENT 4: Yeh, Mike. Talk about put-downs. He puts a new bottom on negative.

STUDENT 3: Hey, I have an idea.

STUDENT 1: What?

STUDENT 3: How about if every time one of them says something negative,

STUDENT 1: WE say something positive to off-balance it.

STUDENT 2-4:YEH!

Pause.

Karl, Ben, and Mike saunter on from right.

KARL: Man, that cafeteria food is awful!

Student 1 moves the marker from 0 to –1 on a posted number line.

BEN: The pits!

Student 1 moves from –1 to –2 on the number line.

STUDENT 3: I thought the pizza was great.

Student 1 moves from –2 to –1 on the number line.

STUDENT 4: The salad was really good.

Student 1 moves from –1 to 0 on the number line.

STUDENT: Have you ever tried their popovers?

STUDENTs 2 & 4: Great:

Student 1 moves from 0 to +2 on the number line.

MIKE: You guys are nuts! Those popovers are so greasy! Yuk!

BEN: Garbage!

Student 1 moves from +2 to 0 on the number line.

STUDENT 1 *whispering*

We're flat even. Let's get ahead.

STUDENT 4: Boy, I learned a lot in Mr. Carlsen's class today.

STUDENT 1: He's one dynamite math teacher!

STUDENT 2: Roger that!

Student 1 moves from 0 to +2 on the number line.

STUDENT 3: He even let us do a readers theatre in class.

Student 1 moves from +2 to +3 on the number line.

MIKE: A what?

STUDENT 3: A readers theatre.

STUDENT 2: You know. You get to do like a little play,

STUDENT 3: but you don't have to memorize or anything.

STUDENT 4: It's a cool way to learn.

Student 1 moves from +3 to + 10 on the number line.

BEN: Never heard of it.

STUDENT 2: That's your loss

STUDENT 1: and our gain.

One, Two Buckle My Shoe
4 Readers

READER 1: This poem requires four readers.

READER 2: Let us introduce ourselves.

READER 1: I am Reader One and my name is _____.

READER 2: I am Reader Two and my name is _____.

READER 3: I am Reader Three and my name is _____.

READER 4: I am Reader Four and my name is _____.

READER 1: We can already count—One, two,

READER 2: three, four

READER 3: five, six,

READER 4: seven, eight.

READER 1: And can even count backwards. Six, five,

READER 2: four, three,

READER 3: two, one.

READER 4: Here is a poem

READER 1: that makes counting

READER 2: fun to listen to.

READER 4: One, two,

ALL: buckle my shoe.

READER 2: Three, four,

ALL: shut the door.

READER 3: Five, six,

ALL: pick up sticks.

READER 1: Seven, eight,

ALL: lay them straight.

READER 3: Nine, ten,

ALL: a good fat hen.

READER 4: Eleven, twelve,

ALL: ring the bells.

READER 2: Thirteen, fourteen,

ALL: maids are courting.

READER 3: Fifteen, sixteen,

ALL: boys are jumping.

READER 2: Seventeen, eighteen,

ALL: kids are waiting.

READER 3: Nineteen, twenty,
ALL: my plate's empty.
READER 1: Have you heard it this way?
ALL: Buckle my shoe,
READER 1: one or two.
ALL: Shut the door,
READER 2: three times or four.
ALL: Pick up sticks,
READER 3: five bundles or six.
ALL: Lay them straight,
READER 4: seven times maybe eight.
ALL: A good fat hen,
READER 3: nine pounds or ten.
ALL: Ring the bells,
READER 1: eleven, twelve.
ALL: Boys are courting,
READER 2: thirteen, are there fourteen?
ALL: Girls are listening,
READER 1: fifteen sometimes sixteen.
ALL: Kids are waiting,
READER 3: seventeen kids, eighteen.
ALL: My platter's empty,
READER 4: nineteen helpings, twenty.
READER 1: We can also count by two.
READER 2: Two-shoes. Four-doors.
READER 4: Six-sticks. Eight-straight.
READER 2: Ten-hens. Twelve-bells.
READER 4: Fourteen-courting. Sixteen-listening.
READER 1: Eighteen-waiting. Twenty-plenty.
READER 1: We can also count by two
READER 2: which will be new to you.
READER 4: One-fun. Three-tree.
READER 2: Five-dive. Seven-heaven.
READER 2: Nine-climb. Eleven-more heaven.
READER 4: Thirteen-twirling.
ALL: Fifteen-lifting.
READER 3: Seventeen-bending.

READER 2: Nineteen-shining.
READER 1: Twenty-one more fun.
ALL: The End.

Shapes

Sing to the tune of "If You're Happy and You Know It"
18 or more Readers/Singers holding cards

READER 1: If you have _____ sides,
ALL: you're a _____.
READER 2: If you have _____ sides,
ALL: you're a _____.
READER 1: If you have _____ sides,
READER 2: Then you surely realize
READER 1: If you have _____ sides,
ALL: you're a _____.

Repeat 9 times, once for each plane geometric figure.
3—triangle
4—quadrilateral
5—pentagon
6—hexagon
7—heptagon
8—octagon
9—nonagon
10—decagon
12—dodecagon

Twinkle Twos

Sing to the tune of "Twinkle, Twinkle, Little Star"
8 Readers: VOICES 1-3, GROUPS A-E

VOICE 1: Start at zero.
VOICE 2: Skip by two.
VOICE 3: I can do it.
VOICES 1, 2,3: So can you!

GROUP A: Zero,
GROUP B: Two,
GROUP C: Four,
GROUP D: Six,
GROUP E: Eight,
ALL: Then start again.

GROUP A: Ten,
GROUP B: Twelve,
GROUP C: Fourteen,
GROUP D: Sixteen,
GROUP E: Eighteen,
ALL: Then start again.

GROUP A: Twenty,
GROUP B: Twenty-two,
GROUP C: Twenty-four,
GROUP D: Twenty-six,
GROUP E: Twenty-eight,
ALL: Then start again.

GROUP A: Thirty,
GROUP B: Thirty-two,
GROUP C: Thirty-four,
GROUP D: Thirty-six,
GROUP E: Thirty-eight,
ALL: Then start again.
Etc.—ninety-eight, then....

ALL *(shouting)*
ONE HUNDRED!

A Vocal Parabola
Entire Class

STUDENTS: 1-36: Oh yeah.
STUDENTS: 1-25: Oh yeah.
STUDENTS: 1-16: Oh yeah.
STUDENTS: 1-9: Oh yeah.
STUDENTS: 1-4: Oh yeah.
STUDENT 1: Oh yeah.
STUDENTS: 1-4: Oh yeah.
STUDENTS: 1-9: Oh yeah.
STUDENTS: 1-16: Oh yeah.
STUDENTS: 1-25: Oh yeah.
STUDENTS: 1-36: Oh yeah.

Presentational End Notes

- Angles—Divide the class into groups of five. Each group can experience reading and learning together. As a culminating experience the entire class could read the angle lines in unison.

- Balloons—Select ten students to perform the scenario. Movement and actions help the audience understand. Next divide the class into cooperative groups. Give each student a copy of the script on which the asterisked numerals have been whited out. Have the students use manipulatives to determine which numbers to fill in. Using this script repeat the RT again, with different students taking the roles.

- How Big is Pi?—We have found that having two students practice the reading a day before presentation makes it more interesting to listen to.

- Negative-Positive Tug of War—Assign parts in advance and allow practice time so the performance runs smoothly. Post a number line from -10 to + 10 stage left so the audience can see it easily. Provide student 1 with a pointer or marker.

  Position Students 1-4 front right and Karl, Ben, and Mike off stage to the right.

  After the presentation, students explain why a negative number added to another number make a larger negative number, why a positive number makes a negative number smaller, etc. In a fifth-grade classroom, students followed up by writing their own RT about borrowing money, more money, and more money, but getting out of the hole by earning money, more money, and more money.

- One Two Buckle My Shoe—Project the reading or provide a copy for each student; then read every other line with the students. Repeat the above but have the students read different lines.

- Shapes—Make shape and numeral cards for all members of the class, minimally 9 with numerals and 9 with cut-outs of shapes.* Use duplicate shape cards as necessary to be sure all participate. On the back of each card, place a copy of the frame. Distribute the cards in random order. Ask students with numeral cards to place themselves in order, in front of the room; it is best to have chairs for these students. Ask those with shape cards to stand directly behind those with matching numerals. The triangle readers/singers begin, completing the frame with "3." The whole class responds with the alternate ("All") lines adding "triangle." Repeat this procedure with each of the 9 shapes.

*Note: A variety of picture cards would fit "quadrilateral": square, rhombus, rectangle, parallelogram, trapezoid. Have fun with it. Bring up 5 at a time for this one; on a repeated run-through, switch cards; or do whatever fits your circumstances.

A transcurricular connection can be made by asking students to investigate the etymology of word parts: -lateral, -gon, tri-, quad-, etc.

- Twinkle Twos—Begin by teaching the song in unison; then prepare manipulatives of the numerals 1-10 (magnetic numerals, plastic numerals, transparency squares). Display this frame.

	0
	2
	4
	6
	8

To create the two-digit numerals as they are sung (or said), place the appropriate tens-place numeral in front of the '0' and slide it down the column to make new numerals. For instance, slide a '1' from the top row down one at a time to make 10, 12, 14, 16, 18. Next use '2' to make 20, 22, 24, 26, 28, and so forth. When you reach 100, you will need to add '10' to the '0.'

Option: After the teacher leads this activity several times on the overhead or a magnetic board, students may use similar manipulatives at their tables or centers. This works well as a partner activity.

Another Option: Use Number Lines. Children face the class number line and watch as the teacher uses a pointer to skip to the numerals, as they are sung/said.

Later children take turns being the pointers.

Eventually, children track on their individual number lines.

- Vocal Parabola—This RT has been used in high school algebra class as an introduction to the lesson. It was designed so that non-mathematical, linguistic students would be able to hear a parabola. Assign a number to each student. As they repeat the simple phrase, 'Oh Yeah' as indicated, the voices make a parabola.

12

Social Studies/History—Sample Scripts

Trying to categorize scripts into various disciplines is not easy, because Readers Theatre (RT) used in science, language arts or even mathematics can often be effectively used in history and geography lessons. As a social studies teacher, please don't just focus on the scripts in this chapter. Peruse the language arts, science and mathematics scripts; you just might find ways to involve your students in creative and enjoyable transcurricular activities with these readings. As a teacher you set the stage for whether a reading will be successful. Feel free to use these scripts in any ways that will enhance student learning.

The alphabetical listing below gives an overview of the content and instructional focus of each script included in this chapter. At the end of the chapter is a matching alphabetical listing of scripts entitled **Presentational End Notes**. They contain our suggestions for ways these RTs could be used in the classroom.

- Annie Oakley—Humanizes a study of the Old West. This script also demonstrates the features of a legend. (Language Arts)

- Boy Who Cried Wolf—Stimulates discussion of the need for honest public servants. This script also demonstrates the key characteristic of a fable, the stating of a moral. (Language Arts)

- Call 911—Introduces and/or reinforces concepts during a unit on Community Workers.

- Colonists and Tea Time—Introduces a unit on the Revolutionary War. Analysis of the reading helps make the events leading up to the war more understandable.

- Columbus' Press Conference—Teaches key facts students should know about the historic trip of Columbus to discover the New World. This tongue-in-cheek conversation among Columbus and three reporters makes 'dry facts' come alive.

- Gettysburg Address Prologue—Sets the stage for discussion of Lincoln's famous address at Gettysburg. The script provides historical background to the events involved in the dedication of a cemetery.

- Gettysburg Address—Allows the students to take this great president's place in history. It can be used as an introduction or summary, but can also serve as a stimulus for discussion as the teacher stops at critical points in this script of Lincoln's famous speech. This RT has been used effectively from grade 5 to adult classes.

- Good Morning, Mr. President—Draws attention to the intriguing coincidences between the lives of Presidents Lincoln and Kennedy. Students always find these facts fascinating.

- Hangin' Chad—Portrays a recent historic event in a humorous style. The presidential election of 2000 was about as exciting as any in American history. For weeks the results were being determined in the courts of the Florida and the Supreme Court of the United States. Much of the controversy surrounded the south Florida ballots with their hanging chads.

- I Have A Dream—Allows students to experience this memorable speech by Martin Luther King, Jr. This reading can be used within a civil rights unit or as a public performance on Martin Luther King, Jr. Day. This script is also a powerful example of persuasive writing. (Language Arts)

- John Henry—Helps students visualize the changes brought about during the U. S. Industrial Revolution. It can be used anywhere with the unit. This script is also a clear example of a legend, with its exaggeration of a folk hero's prowess. (Language Arts)

- Liberty or Death—Gives students an opportunity to relive Patrick Henry's famous speech.

- Old Rat's Tale—Provides a good introduction to a unit on exploration. This script also gives opportunity to review the meanings of homophones. (Language Arts)

- Susanna—Provides an historical perspective on women's issues and rights during the days of antiquity.

- There's Only One 'I'—Serves as a chant/theme song for a unit on responsibility.

- These Things Called Maps—Describes just what maps do for us. At the end of the reading the text changes; we are no longer looking at actual maps but at metaphorical maps. This reading can be used to introduce or culminate a lesson on maps and compasses. It also provides good opportunity for a transcurricular connection, as students feel the shift from fact to metaphor. (Language Arts)

- Three Billy Goats Gruff—Symbolizes power struggles. This folk tale can be used anywhere within social studies classes, because power play has been at the heart of virtually all conflicts throughout history. As a transcurricular activity, students can compare and contrast the plot lines in various versions of this tale. (Language Arts)

Annie Oakley

13 Readers: NARRATORS 1-8, MA, PA, ANNIE, FRANK, BUFFALO BILL

MA: *Muttering.*
Where is that girl?
PA: She was out past the barn last I saw her.
MA: Well, I'll be. I told her she was to wash these dishes. She's nine now. She should be workin', not playin'!
Pause.
MA: Well, there you are, Annie. Where've you been?
ANNIE: Fetchin' us some supper.
PA: Well, I'll be. A rabbit.
ANNIE: <u>Two</u> rabbits. You get after these, Ma, and I'll get after those dishes.

NARRATOR 1: Five years later, when Annie was 14
PA: Annie, you've made your family mighty proud!
ANNIE: Did you do it, Pa?! Did you really do it?!
PA: Yep. Here it is. Paid in full. No more mortgage hangin' over our heads!
MA: Annie, I never did cotton much to all that shootin' practice, but it sure has paid off.
ANNIE: I can't even remember how many contests it took, but the important thing is—the mortgage is paid off.
PA: Annie, you're our rootin'-tootin'-shootin' sweetheart!
NARRATOR 2: One year later, in 1875, when Annie was 15
MA: *Calling as to a far off place.*
Pa, come on in. Annie's home.
PA: *Cautiously.*
Annie, Annie, how'd it go?
ANNIE: Oh, Ma, it was fabulous! Vaudeville shows are amazing!
MA: But the contest, Annie, the contest.
ANNIE: I won.
MA: Pa, Pa, she won! She beat Frank Butler!
PA: *Amazed.*
Really?!! Never in a million moons…
ANNIE: Would you like to meet Frank Butler?
PA: What?
ANNIE: He's comin' to visit, as soon has he's finished in Cinncinnati. He's comin' here.

NARRATOR 3: Frank Butler did visit the Oakleys.

NARRATOR 4: Later he married Annie and became her manager.

FRANK: I've found you a steady job, Annie.

ANNIE: Really?

FRANK: We're heading out to join up with the Sells Brothers' Circus.

ANNIE: Oh, Frank, this is wonderful!

FRANK: Yep.

ANNIE: We won't have to wonder where and when the next contest will be.

FRANK: Nope.

ANNIE: I'll be working every day.

FRANK: Yep, and you'll be a regular attraction, just showing off you stuff!

NARRATOR 5: Annie was so good she drew the attention of every marksman in the West.

NARRATOR 6: One day Frank gave her more important news.

FRANK: Annie, who has the best show in the West?

ANNIE: Buffalo Bill.

FRANK: Yep. Would you like to meet him?

ANNIE: Meet Buffalo Bill? That would be such an honor!

FRANK: Come on outside, Annie

BUFFALO BILL: Annie, I'm glad to meet you. I'm a great admirer of yours.

ANNIE: *Incredulously.*

You admire me!? Why, I admire you!

BUFFALO BILL: Then we should make a great team. How would you like to become part of Buffalo Bill's Wild West Show?

NARRATOR 7: Of course Annie said 'Yes' before nearly fainting away with surprise.

NARRATOR 8: And for 17 years she was known as

ALL EXCEPT ANNIE: THE GREATEST MARKSMAN IN THE WEST!

Boy Who Cried Wolf—Aesop's Fable

12 Readers: NARRATORS 1-7, BOY, MAN, WOMAN, GIRL, AUDIENCE (as the townspeople).
(MAN, WOMAN, and GIRL are part of the townspeople; they should therefore join in on the AUDIENCE parts.)

NARRATOR 1: Once upon a time
NARRATOR 2: there was a shepherd boy
NARRATOR 3: who spent every day
NARRATOR 4: staring at the sheep,
NARRATOR 5: *Slower.*
staring at the sheep,
NARRATOR 6: *Slower.*
staring at the sheep,
NARRATOR 7: *Slower.*
and staring at the sheep!
NARRATOR 1: One day
NARRATOR 2: he decided to have some fun.
NARRATOR 3: He ran headlong
NARRATOR 4: down the hill,
NARRATOR 5: *Faster.*
down the hill,
NARRATOR 6: *Faster.*
down the hill,
NARRATOR 7: *Faster.*
down the hill,
NARRATOR 2: crying—
BOY: Wolf! Wolf! Wolf!
NARRATOR 3: From all over town,
NARRATOR 1: the sheep owners,
NARRATOR 2: their wives,
NARRATOR 3: their children,
NARRATORS 1,2,3: <u>everyone</u> ran
NARRATOR 4: up the hill,
NARRATOR 5: *Slower.*
up the hill,
NARRATOR 6: *Slower.*
up the hill,

NARRATOR 7: *Slower.*
up the hill,
NARRATOR 3: to protect their sheep.
NARRATOR 1: All the while
NARRATOR 2: the boy cried:
BOY: Wolf! Wolf! Wolf!
NARRATOR 3: When they came to the top of the hill,
NARRATOR 1: the people shouted:
AUDIENCE: Where?! Where?! Where?!
NARRATOR 2: But no one saw a wolf.
MAN: I don't see any wolf.
WOMAN: I don't see any wolf.
GIRL: I don't see any wolf.
AUDIENCE: I don't see any wolf.
BOY: It ran away.
AUDIENCE: That's good.
BOY: It must have been all the noise. Thank you.
AUDIENCE You're welcome.

NARRATOR 1: All was well for a while,
NARRATOR 2: but one day,
NARRATOR 3: as the shepherd boy
NARRATOR 4: stared at the sheep,
NARRATOR 5: *Slower.*
stared at the sheep,
NARRATOR 6: *Slower.*
stared at the sheep
NARRATOR 7: *Slower.*
and stared at the sheep,
NARRATOR 1: he again became bored.
NARRATOR 2: Once again be cried:
BOY: Wolf! Wolf! Wolf!
NARRATOR 3: From all over town,
NARRATOR 1: the sheep owners,
NARRATOR 2: their wives,
NARRATOR 3: their children,
NARRATORS1,2,3: <u>everyone</u> ran
NARRATOR 4: up the hill,

NARRATOR 5: *Slower.*
up the hill,
NARRATOR 6: *Slower.*
up the hill,
NARRATOR 7: *Slower.*
up the hill
NARRATOR 2: to protect their sheep.
NARRATOR 3: When they came to the top of the hill,
NARRATOR 1: the people shouted:
AUDIENCE: Where?! Where?! Where?!
NARRATOR 2: But no one saw a wolf.
MAN: I don't see any wolf.
WOMAN: I don't see any wolf.
GIRL: I don't see any wolf.
AUDIENCE: I don't see any wolf.
BOY: It ran away!
NARRATOR 2: The people sighed with relief
NARRATOR 3: and went back home.
NARRATOR 1: But then they began to talk among themselves.
WOMAN: When the wolf came, did you lose any sheep?
MAN: I didn't lose any.
GIRL: I didn't lose any.
AUDIENCE: We didn't lose any.
MAN: This is most curious.
AUDIENCE Most curious indeed!
WOMAN: Either that wolf was very slow
GIRL: or very stupid,
AUDIENCE: **Slowly.**
OR....!
Pause.
NARRATOR 1: Some days later
NARRATOR 2: as the shepherd boy was watching the sheep,
NARRATOR 3: he looked up
NARRATOR 1: and saw...
NARRATORS 1,2,3: a **Wolf!**
NARRATOR 1: Once again he cried:
BOY: Wolf! Wolf! Wolf!
NARRATOR 1: But no one ran up the hill,

NARRATOR 4: no one,
NARRATOR 5: no one,
NARRATOR 6: no one,
NARRATOR 7: no one.
NARRATOR 2: No one saved the sheep.
NARRATOR 1: And this time the boy cried,
NARRATOR 2: and cried,
NARRATOR 3: and cried.
BOY: Wolf! Wolf! Wolf!
NARRATOR 2: And no one saved the boy.
Pause.
ALL (except BOY): **A liar is not believed, even when he tells the truth.**

Call 911

5 Readers: SOLO VOICES and AUDIENCE

ALL: HELP! HELP!
VOICE 1: My house is on fire!
ALL: Call 911!
VOICE 2: Hurry, Mr. Squire!

ALL: HELP! HELP!
VOICE 3: My sister's in the pool!
ALL: Call 911!
VOICE 4: Hurry, Miss O'Toole!

ALL: HELP! HELP!
VOICE 5: A robber took my bike!
ALL: Call 911!
VOICE 5: Hurry, Mrs. Pike!
All make siren noises.
ALL: Here they come!
VOICES 1, 2, 3: Heroes of the day!
VOICE 1: The fire is out!
VOICE 3: My sister's fine!
VOICE 5: They hauled the thief away!

VOICE 2: Firemen,
VOICE 4: Doctors,
VOICE 5: Wonderful Policemen!
VOICE 1: The fire is out.
VOICE 3: My sister's fine.
VOICE 5: And my bike is back again!

VOICE 2: Thank you!
VOICE 4: Thank you!
VOICES 1-5: Heroes of the day!
ALL: **Thank you! Thank you! HURRAY! HURRAY!**

Colonist and Tea Time

6 Readers: CARL, COLIN THE COLONIST, TOM THE TAX COLLECTOR, KING'S REP 1 & 2, KING

CARL: What?

COLIN: New Taxes?

TOM: You got that right.

CARL: I can't believe this.

COLIN: Here is the bill; seeing is believing.

CARL: The King has some nerve.

TOM: The King is King. What can I say?

CARL: We have lived on this continent, how many years now?

COLIN: At least, one hundred.

TOM: True, but how much tax have you paid?

CARL: Paid taxes for what?

COLIN: Food stamps?

CARL: A health care plan?

COLIN: Oh, I know. It's for social security.

CARL: I've got a better one. The tax will pay for foreign aid to England.

TOM: Let's not fight over this. Just pay up.

COLIN: Who do you guys in parliament think you are?

TOM: They are the lawmakers and the taxers.

CARL: It is easy for you to make laws for us.

COLIN: Hello, Colonist.

CARL: Good morning, Americans.

COLIN: You owe us some money.

CARL: Whatever you say, your Lordship!

COLIN: Yea, what do you want?

CARL: The King and Parliament need to wake up.

COLIN: Yea, wake up and smell the tea.

TOM: That is exactly what has happened.

CARL: You say what?

TOM: I have come to collect the King's taxes on tea.

COLIN: Oh, get a grip.

CARL: I refuse to pay.

COLIN: He can't make us pay.

TOM: Remember, the King is king.

CARL: And you remember

COLIN: You are here and he is there.

CARL: Those fools in Parliament have voted this tax on us.

TOM: Look!

COLIN: We don't have any say.

TOM: This is my job to collect the taxes. Don't give me a hard time.

CARL: You...

COLIN: ...you are going to keep some of the taxes for yourself, you traitor!

TOM: Well, I have to live you know.

CARL: You'd better move along before we tar and feather you.

TOM: Wait, I am one of the King's men!

COLIN: So you are a Tory!

CARL: Where does your loyalty lie,

COLIN: with the King or with your fellow Americans?

TOM: It lies with whoever puts food on my table.

CARL: You are a man of real and rare principles!

TOM: You are the ones who are traitors, traitors to the crown of England.

COLIN: Oh come on!

CARL: If the King does not respect us as colonists by giving us a voice in Parliament,

COLIN: we will not respect him or his bloody taxes!

TOM: Watch your language.

CARL: This is tyranny!

TOM: Maybe you need to hear the King's side of the tax story.

COLIN: Yeh, I would like to hear that all right.

TOM: Listen in to this conversation and maybe you will pay your taxes.

KING'S REP 2: O King, we are broke!

KING: Broke...as in no money?

KING'S REP 1: The French and Indian War have depleted our funds.

KING'S REP 2: We got a lot of land

KING'S REP 1: But now we have no money.

KING: In order to maintain the English empire I need more money.

KING'S REP 2: What should we do?

KING'S REP 1: That blasted war gave us more land than we can use.

KING: We now have Canada!

KING'S REP 2: and all the French holdings east of the Mississippi.

KING'S REP 1: War cost so much money!

KING: And now we have no more money in the treasury?

KING'S REP 2: The colonialists in America will benefit
KING'S REP 1: from all the new land that we have gained.
KING'S REP 2: But the British government will see no money from it.
KING'S REP 1: Why don't we have the colonials
KING'S REP 2: bear their fair share of the financial burden?!

KING: Excellent! Parliament. Pass new taxes.
KING'S REP 1: At your command, oh, King.
KING: They can help refill our treasury.
KING'S REP 2: It is their war that put us in this predicament in the first place.
KING: Tax their tea!
KING'S REP 2: But...
KING'S REP 1: but what if they switch to coffee drinking?
KING: Tax the tea and then the coffee if we have to.
CARL: I have an idea.
COLIN: Let's have a tea party in Boston.

Columbus' Press Conference

4 Readers: REPORTER 1,2,3, COLUMBUS

REPORTER 1: Christopher Columbus is slated to have a news conference this morning.

REPORTER 2: We are aboard his ship Santa Maria

REPORTER 3: getting ready for his trip into the unknown sea.

REPORTER 2: While we are waiting for Admiral Columbus a little background is in order.

REPORTER 3: The year is 1492.

REPORTER 1: Most know that Columbus jumped ship,

REPORTER 3: pardon the pun,

REPORTER 2: by sailing under a Spanish flag.

REPORTER 1: Columbus is actually from Italy

REPORTER 3: but got funding from the King of Spain, Ferdinand,

REPORTER 2: and from the Queen of Spain, Isabel.

REPORTER 1: Hopefully Columbus will appear any time now.

REPORTER 3: Look. There he is talking to the men of his ship.

REPORTER 2: He has probably forgotten his press conference.

REPORTER 1: He looks busy.

REPORTER 3: Never mind. We must get this story for the Madrid Inquirer.

COLUMBUS: Come on men. Let's get this ship moving faster.

REPORTER 1: Admiral Columbus…

COLUMBUS: Pull up another sail!

REPORTER 1: Sir…

COLUMBUS: Quit that sleeping on deck and get to your duties.

REPORTER 2: Hello…

COLUMBUS: We've got to discover the New World.

REPORTER 2: Your press conference.

COLUMBUS: I know. You're cold and hungry.

REPORTER 3: Excuse me, sir.

COLUMBUS: This voyage is a hardship for all of us,

REPORTER 3: Chris…

COLUMBUS: but think of the adventure of it and the great service

REPORTER 1: Chris…

COLUMBUS: you'll be doing for mankind by proving the world is round.

REPORTER 1: We had an appointment with…

COLUMBUS: You are all great sailors, men,

REPORTER 1: Sir.

COLUMBUS: and you and our ship will never be forgotten

REPORTER 2: Sir, Sir.

COLUMBUS: because we set forth with courage and faith to discover the New World.

ALL REPORTERS: Admiral Christopher Columbus!

COLUMBUS: Oh, pardon me, young men.

REPORTER 1: Could we have a word with you?

COLUMBUS: I didn't know you were around.

ALL REPORTERS: We are from the Madrid Inquirer.

COLUMBUS: Why didn't you speak up so I knew you were around?

REPORTER 1: Well, we...

COLUMBUS: Speak up. I will answer any questions.

REPORTER 2: You have been giving an enthusiastic challenge

REPORTER 3: to your sailors on this long trip.

REPORTER 1: How long have you been out to sea?

COLUMBUS: Fifteen minutes.

ALL REPORTERS: Fifteen minutes!

REPORTER 3: How do you handle being away from home out on the ocean.

REPORTER 2: for such a long period of time?

COLUMBUS: Well, it's because I love the sea,

REPORTER 2: and

COLUMBUS: it's a long way to the new world.

REPORTER 3: You don't know where you are going, do you?

COLUMBUS: Wherever this ship takes me. I love this ship.

REPORTER 3: That's very romantic.

COLUMBUS: I'm married to this ship.

REPORTER 2: That's heavy!

COLUMBUS: She's the finest wife a man could ever have!

REPORTER 3: Oh, by the way,

REPORTER 2: what are those other two ships

REPORTER 1: following along behind?

COLUMBUS: Those are the kids. We call them Pinta and Nina.

REPORTER 2: Cute little rascals!

COLUMBUS: They take after their mother.

REPORTER 2: Their mother?

COLUMBUS: The Santa Maria, of course.

REPORTER 2: Chris...

REPORTER 1: do you mind if we call you Chris?
COLUMBUS: I certainly do mind! It is Admiral Columbus.
REPORTER 1: Sorry, Admiral.
REPORTER 2: What compels a man of your character
REPORTER 3: to set sail for the purpose of discovering the New World?
COLUMBUS: Poetry.
REPORTER 1: Poetry!
COLUMBUS: It's because I like poetry.
REPORTER 3: Please explain, sir.
COLUMBUS: I write poetry you see.
REPORTER 2: I thought you wanted to discover the New World.
COLUMBUS: I'm not much concerned about what I discover.
REPORTER 3: Really!
COLUMBUS: I just want a poem.
REPORTER 3: You just want a poem?
COLUMBUS: Oh, just a simple little poem about me.
REPORTER 2: Of course. Who else!?
COLUMBUS: A poem all school kids could memorize, to remember my name.
REPORTER 1: Can you quote some of the lines?
COLUMBUS: I've been doing some writing.
REPORTER 1: We're listening.
COLUMBUS: In fourteen hundred and eighty-three, Columbus sailed as fast as a bee.
REPORTER 3: That's it?
COLUMBUS: It's a start. Do you have other suggestions?
REPORTER 1: Well—
COLUMBUS: It's got to have a ring to it.
REPORTER 1: What about this.
REPORTER 2: In fourteen hundred and eighty-three,
REPORTER 3: Beneath the swaying chestnut tree.
COLUMBUS: That's it! That's great! You've got the idea.
REPORTER 3: Thank you.
COLUMBUS: But you left my name out again!
REPORTER 3: Sorry!
COLUMBUS: Do you have another one?
REPORTER 2: In fourteen hundred and eighty-three,
REPORTER 1: Columbus
REPORTER 2: exhibited his gallantry.

REPORTER 3: It has all the essentials.

COLUMBUS: Not quite the ring needed.

REPORTER 2: I've got one.

REPORTER 3: In fourteen hundred and eighty-three,

REPORTER 1: upon the ship, upon the sea,

REPORTER 2: in the midst of the storm always courageous

REPORTER 3: was our sailor, never forlorn.

COLUMBUS: You left my name out again.

REPORTER 3: Oh!

COLUMBUS: And it is too long.

REPORTER 2: Just trying to be helpful.

COLUMBUS: In fourteen hundred and eighty-three, Columbus is the boy for me.

REPORTER 2: Sir, I don't think school kids

REPORTER 3: will remember that one.

REPORTER 1: Here's one more.

REPORTER 2: In fourteen hundred and ninety-two

REPORTER 3: Columbus sailed the ocean blue.

COLUMBUS: That's exactly what I've been looking for!

REPORTER 1: But Admiral Columbus,

REPORTER 3: the year 1492 is nine years from now.

COLUMBUS: Who cares! All I want is a poem. Okay, men, we're turning around!

REPORTER 3: Go back toward Spain?

COLUMBUS: We'll come back in nine years!

REPORTER 2: Some story! Headlines...

REPORTER 3: In fourteen hundred and ninety-two,

REPORTER 1: Columbus will sail the ocean blue.

COLUMBUS: I just love press conferences.

Gettysburg Address Prologue

2 Readers

READER 1: The battle of Gettysburg,

READER 2: the turning point of the Civil War,

READER 1: occurred in July, 1863.

READER 2: The grounds were consecrated

READER 1: as a new cemetery in November of that same year.

READER 2: Edward Everett was asked to give the principal oration.

READER 1: He was a noted preacher,

READER 2: a professor of Greek,

READER 1: a president of Harvard,

READER 2: a United States Senator,

READER 1: a Secretary of State.

READER 2: Abraham Lincoln was also asked to give

READER 1: a few appropriate remarks.

READER 2: He attended school less than one year.

READER 1: He was a log splitter

READER 2: a lawyer,

READER 1: a representative,

READER 2: and President of the United States.

READER 1: Everett's long oration was given by heart.

READER 2: Lincoln's short address was given from the heart.

READER 1: And now the Gettysburg Address by Abraham Lincoln.

Gettysburg Address

By Abraham Lincoln adapted for Readers Theatre
4 Readers

READER 1: Fourscore and seven years ago
READER 2: our fathers
READER 3: brought forth on this continent a new nation,
READER 4: conceived in liberty
READER 2: and dedicated to the proposition
READER 3: that all men are created equal.

READER 1: Now we are engaged in a great civil war,
READER 4: testing whether that nation
READER 3: or any nation
READER 4: so conceived
READER 1: and so dedicated can long endure.
READER 2: We are met on a great battlefield of that war.

READER 4: We have come to dedicate a portion of that field
READER 3: as a final resting-place
READER 1: for those who here gave their lives
READER 2: that that nation might live.
READER 3: It is altogether fitting
READER 4: and proper that we should do this.

READER 1: But in a larger sense,
READER 3: we cannot dedicate,
READER 2: we cannot consecrate,
READER 4: we cannot hallow this ground.
READER 2: The brave men,
READER 3: living and dead
READER 1: who struggled here
READER 4: have consecrated it far above
READER 2: our poor power to add or detract.
READER 3: The world will little note
READER 2: nor long remember what we say here,
READER 1: but it can never forget
READER 4: what they did here.

READER 2: It is for us the living
READER 4: rather to be dedicated here to the unfinished work
READER 2: which they who fought here
READER 3: have thus far so nobly advanced.
READER 4: It is rather for us
READER 1: to be here dedicated to the great task remaining before us—
READER 2: that from these honored dead
READER 3: we take increased devotion
READER 4: to that cause for which they gave the last full measure of devotion—
READER 2: that we here highly resolve
READER 1: that these dead
READER 3: shall not have died in vain,
READER 4: that this nation under God
READER 1: shall have a new birth of freedom,
READER 2: and that government
READER 4: of the people,
READER 3: by the people,
READER 1: for the people
READER 4: shall not perish from the earth.

Good Morning, Mr. President—A Two-Century Press Conference

Entire Class:
ANDREW JOHNSON, PUB REL DIR 1, REPORTERS 1-5 (& EXTRA
REPORTERS) ON SIDE 1;
LYNDON JOHNSON, PUB REL DIR 2, REPORTERS 6-10 (& EXTRA
REPORTERS) ON SIDE 2

PUB REL DIR 1: Good morning, Mr. President.
ANDREW JOHNSON: Good morning.
PUB REL DIR 1: The events of the past 24 hours have changed the course of history. The President will answer a few questions before undertaking the difficult tasks that now lie ahead for him.

REPORTER 1: How does it feel to be addressed as Mr. President?
ANDREW JOHNSON: Sad, sad. Yesterday was the darkest of Fridays.
SIDE 1REPORTERS: The darkest of Fridays.

PUB REL DIR 2: Good morning, Mr. President.
LYNDON JOHNSON: Good morning.
PUB REL DIR 2: The events of the past 24 hours have changed the course of history. The President will answer a few questions before undertaking the difficult tasks that now lie ahead for him.
REPORTER 6: How does it feel to be addressed as Mr. President?
LYNDON OHNSON: Sad, sad. Yesterday was the darkest of Fridays.
SIDE 2 REPORTERS: The darkest of Fridays.

REPORTER 2: Was there any foreboding, any premonition that Mr. Lincoln would be assassinated?
ANDREW JOHNSON: In actuality, there was. His secretary, Ms. Kennedy, cautioned him against going to the theater. She said she felt it unwise.
SIDE 1REPORTERS: Most unwise.

REPORTER 7: Was there any foreboding, any premonition that Mr. Kennedy would be assassinated?

LYNDON JOHNSON: In actuality, there was. His secretary, Ms. Johnson, cautioned him against going to the Dallas. She said she felt it unwise.
SIDE 2 REPORTERS: Most unwise.

REPORTER 3: What went through your mind when you learned of Mr. Lincoln's death?
ANDREW JOHNSON: My first thought was, Oh, what a horrible experience for his wife, holding him in her arms as blood poured from that shot in the back of his head!
REPORTER 3: And then?
ANDREW JOHNSON: A strange irony crossed my mind. When he was 23 years old, Abe joined the armed forces to defend his country. Now he has been destroyed by a coward from among his own people.
SIDE 1 REPORTERS: Coward.

REPORTER 8: What went through your mind when you learned of Mr. Lincoln's death?
LYNDON JOHNSON: My first thought was, Oh, what a horrible experience for his wife, holding him in her arms as blood poured from that shot in the back of his head!
REPORTER 8: And then?
LYNDON JOHNSON: A strange irony crossed my mind. When he was 23 years old, Jack joined the armed forces to defend his country. Now he has been destroyed by a coward from among his own people.
SIDE 2 REPORTERS: Coward.

REPORTER 4: We have heard reports that the assassin was a John Wilkes Booth who fled from the theater at which he shot President Lincoln and disappeared into a warehouse.
ANDREW JOHNSON: This is the unconfirmed report.
SIDE 1 REPORTERS: Coward.

REPORTER 9: We have heard reports that the assassin was a Lee Harvey Oswald who fled from the warehouse from which he shot President Kennedy and disappeared into a theater.
LYNDON JOHNSON: This is the unconfirmed report.
SIDE 2 REPORTERS: Coward.

REPORTER 5: Knowing that President Lincoln's passionate interest in civil rights was likely the reason for his assassination, how vigorously will you pursue this cause?

ANDREW JOHNSON: When Abe was elected in 1860, he committed himself to equal treatment of and opportunities for all men. In his name I will continue to move civil rights efforts forward.

SIDE 1 REPORTERS: Equality for all men.

REPORTER 10: Knowing that President Kennedy's passionate interest in civil rights was likely the reason for his assassination, how vigorously will you pursue this cause?

LYNDON JOHNSON: When Jack was elected in 1960, he committed himself to equal treatment of and opportunities for all men. In his name I will continue to move civil rights efforts forward.

SIDE 2 REPORTERS: Equality for all men.

Hangin' Chad

By Tony Kaspereen
4 Readers: CHAD 1,2; FRIEND 1,2

FRIEND 1: Hey, Chad, what's up?

CHAD 1: Not much—just hangin'.

FRIEND 2: Just hangin', Chad?

CHAD 2: Yep, just hangin'.

FRIEND 2: So, what's new, Chad?

CHAD 1: Ah, spent some time down in Florida.

FRIEND 1: Oh yeah, Chad?

FRIEND 2: Hangin' in Florida?

CHAD 1,2: Yep, just hangin' in Florida.

FRIEND 1: What happened in Florida?

CHAD 2: Oh, you know, just got beat up.

FRIEND 2: Ya got beat up cuz you were just hangin' in Florida, Chad?

CHAD 1: Nah, I didn't start hangin' 'til I got punched.

FRIEND 1: You got punched in Florida, Chad, and then, started hangin'?

CHAD 1: Yep, I was just hangin' in Florida after gettin punched.

FRIEND 2: Hey, Chad, did they hurt ya?

CHAD 1: Nah, they were old people.

FRIEND 1: So?

CHAD 2: Old people don't punch very hard

CHAD 1: so I didn't fall to the ground.—I just started hangin'

CHAD 2: after I got punched by the seniors.

FRIEND 1: That's weird, Chad.

CHAD 2: Know what's even weirder?

FRIEND 2: What's that, Chad?

CHAD 1: Those old people hit me in the stomach.

FRIEND 1: Yeah Chad?

CHAD 2: Well, I got pretty swollen.

FRIEND 2: Yeah Chad?

CHAD 1: Some people thought I was pregnant.

FRIEND 1: Pregnant, Chad?

CHAD 1: Yeah, pregnant.

FRIEND 2: So people thought you were pregnant, Chad,

FRIEND 1: when really you were just hangin', Chad?

CHAD 1,2: Yep, just hangin'.

FRIEND 2: So let me get this all straight, Chad.
FRIEND 1: You were just hangin' in Florida, Chad,
FRIEND 2: and some old people punched you—but not hard.
FRIEND 1: So you just kept hangin', Chad?
CHAD 1: Yep, just hangin'.
Friend 2: Hey Chad—Yeah?
FRIEND 1: Why would old people punch you?
CHAD 1: Maybe cuz I'm cute.
FRIEND 2: That's true.
FRIEND 1: You are dimpled, Chad!
CHAD 2: True.
CHAD 1: I'm just a dimpled, hangin' Chad.
FRIEND 1: Hey Chad—Yeah?
FRIEND 2: Are you?
CHAD 1: Am I?
FRIEND 1: Yeah, are you?
CHAD 2: Am I what?
FRIEND 1: Are you pregnant Chad?
CHAD 1,2: What???!!!
FRIEND 1: Are you?
FRIEND 2: Are you pregnant, Chad?
CHAD 1: No, I'm just hangin'.
FRIEND 1: Just hangin', Chad?
CHAD 1,2: Yep, just hangin'.
FRIEND 1: Hey Chad—Yeah?
FRIEND 2: Think you'll ever head back down to Florida?
CHAD 2: Maybe in like another four years.

I Have A Dream

By Martin Luther King adapted for Readers Theatre
6 Readers: READERS 1,2,3,4; KINGS 1,2

Prologue

READER 1: Five score years ago, a great American, in whose symbolic shadow we stand, signed the Emancipation Proclamation.

READER 2: Five score years ago, this momentous decree came as a great beacon of light to millions of Negro slaves,

READER 1: Five score years ago a decree was given that would be the basis of putting out the searing flames of withering injustice.

READER 2: Five score years ago, it came as a joyous daybreak to end the long night of captivity.

History

READER 1: One hundred years later—

KING 1: The Negro is still not free.

KING 2: The life of the Negro is still sadly crippled.

KING 4: Crippled by manacles of segregation and the chains of discrimination.

KING 3: The Negro lives on a lonely island of poverty.

KING 4: He lives in this poverty in the midst of a vast ocean of material prosperity.

READER 2: One hundred years later—

KING 1: The Negro is still anguished.

KING 2: Anguished in the corners of American society.

KING 3: An exile in his own land.

KING 4: We have come to our Nation's Capital to cash a check.

READER 1: One hundred years later—

KING 3: The Negro has come to fall heir to a promissory note of the Constitution and the Declaration of Independence.

KING 1: We claim the promise that all men,

KING 2: black men and white men,

KING 4: would be guaranteed the unalienable rights.

ALL: Life, liberty and the pursuit of happiness.

READER 2: One hundred years later—

KING 1: America has defaulted on this promissory note.

KING 2: America has defaulted on this sacred obligation.

KING 3: America has given the Negro a bad check. America has given the Negro a check marked

ALL: **insufficient funds.**

READER 1: One hundred years later—

KING 3: America refuses to believe that the bank of justice is bankrupt.

KING 4: America refuses to believe that there are insufficient funds in the great vaults of opportunity.

READER 2: One hundred years later—

KING 1: We have come to remind America of the fierce urgency

KING 2: and that now is the time.

Action

READER 1: Now is the time—

KING 1: To remind America to make real the promises of Democracy.

KING 2: To remind America to rise from segregation.

READER 2: Now is the time—

KING 1: To remind America to rise to the sunlit path of racial justice.

KING 2: To lift our nation from the quicksand of racial injustice.

READER 2: Now is the time—

KING 1: To lift our nation to the solid rock of brotherhood.

KING 2: To make justice the reality for all of God's children.

READER 1: Now is the time—

KING 1: To shake the foundations of our Nation until the bright day of justice emerges.

KING 2: In our struggles for freedom

KING 1: we cannot walk with bitterness and hatred.

KING 2: We cannot walk

KING 1: with physical violence.

KING 2: We cannot walk

KING 1: without our white brothers.

KING 2: As we walk we cannot turn back.

KING 1: We cannot be satisfied

KING 3: as long as the Negro is the victim of unspeakable horrors.

KING 1: We cannot be satisfied

KING 3: as long as our bodies, heavy with the fatigue of travel,

KING 4: cannot gain lodging in the motels and hotels of America.

KING 1: We cannot be satisfied

KING 2: as long as the Negro's basic mobility is from a smaller ghetto to a larger one.

KING 1: As long as our children are stripped of their self-hood.

KING 2: We cannot be satisfied

KING 1: as long as our children are robbed of their dignity,

KING 2: as long as signs says

ALL: **white only.**

KING 1: As long as a Negro in Mississippi cannot vote,

KING 2: as long as a Negro in New York believes he has nothing for which to vote,

ALL: we are not satisfied.

KING 2: No, no, we <u>will not be</u> satisfied,

KING 1: until justice rolls down like water

KING 2: and righteousness like a mighty stream.

Trials

KING 1: I am not unmindful that some of you

KING 2: have come here out of great trials and tribulations.

KING 1: Some of you have come fresh from narrow jail cells.

KING 2: Some of you have come from persecution.

KING 1: Some of you have come from the winds of police brutality.

KING 2: Some of you have come as veterans of creative suffering.

KING 1: All of you have come with a faith that will continue to work.

KING 2: So go back!

KING 1: Go back—To Mississippi?

KING 2: To Alabama?

KING 1: To South Carolina?

KING 2: To Georgia?

KING 1: To Louisiana?

KING 2: Yes, go back!

KING 1: Go back—To the slums and ghettos?

KING 2: Go back—Somehow this situation can and will be changed!

KING 1: Let us not wallow in the valley of despair.

Future

KING 2: I have a dream!

ALL: Even though we face difficulties?

KING 2: I have a dream of today and tomorrow!

KING 1: It is a dream deeply rooted

KING 2: in the American dream.

ALL: We all have a dream.

KING 2: I have a dream that one day this nation will rise up,

KING 1: this nation will live out, the true meaning of this creed:

ALL: We hold these truths to be self-evident,

KING 1: all men are created equal.

ALL: We too have this dream.

KING 2: I have a dream that one day

KING 1: the sons of former slaves,

KING 2: the sons of former slave owners?

KING 1: will be able to sit down together at the table of brotherhood.

ALL: We have that dream.

KING 2: I have a dream that one day,

KING 1: the sweltering heat of injustice and oppression

KING 2: will be transformed into an oasis of freedom and justice.

KING 1: I have a dream that one day my four little children will live

KING 2: in a nation where they will not be judged

KING 1: By the color of their skin but by the content of their character.

KING 2: I have a dream that one day little black boys and black girls

KING 1: and little white boys and white girls will join hands as brothers and sisters.

KING 2: I have a dream that one day every valley shall be exalted,

KING 1: every hill made low, the rough places made plain,

KING 2: the crooked places made straight.

KING 4: Then the glory of the Lord shall be revealed,

KING 3: all flesh shall see it together.

ALL: We all have that dream.

KING 3: This is our hope.

KING 4: This is our faith.

KING 2: With this faith,

KING 1: we will be able to hew out the mountain of despair—the stone of hope.

READER 2: With this faith,
KING 3: we will transform the discords of our nation.
READER 1: With this faith,
KING 4: we will be able to work together.
KING 2: We will pray together.
KING 1: We will struggle together.
KING 2: We will go to jail together.
KING 4: We will stand up for freedom together.
KING 3: Together we will be free one day.
ALL: We all want to be free one day.
KING 1: This is our day—
KING 2: When all of God's people will be able to sing with new meaning
ALL: *All sing together.*
My country 'tis of thee,
Sweet land of liberty, of thee I sing.
Land where my fathers died,
Land of the pilgrim's pride.

Ring of Freedom

KING 2: If America is to be a great nation then let freedom ring
KING 1: from every mountainside,
ALL: Let freedom ring.
KING 1: from the prodigious hilltops of New Hampshire.
KING 2: Let freedom ring,
KING 1: from the mighty mountains of New York.
ALL: Let freedom ring,
KING 3: from the heightening Alleghenies of Pennsylvania.
KING 4: Let freedom ring,
KING 1: from the snowcapped Rockies of Colorado.
ALL: Let freedom ring,
KING 2: from the curvaceous slopes of California.
KING 1: Let freedom ring,
KING 2: from Stone Mountain of Georgia.
ALL: Let freedom ring,
KING 3: from Lookout Mountain of Tennessee.
KING 4: Let freedom ring,
KING 2: from every hill and mole hill of Mississippi.

KING 1: Let freedom ring,

KING 2: from every mountainside.

ALL: Let freedom ring!

KING 2: And when this happens—

ALL: We will be free at last.

KING 3: When we let it ring from every village and every hamlet,

KING 4: when we let it ring from every state and every city

ALL: **finally**—

KING 2: All of God's children,

KING 1: black men and white men,

KING 3: Jews and Gentiles,

KING 4: Protestants and Catholics,

KING 2: will join hands and sing in the words of the old Negro spiritual:

KING 1: Free at last!

KING 2: Free at last! Thank God almighty,

KING 1: we are free at last!

ALL: We are free at last.

KING 2: I have a dream.

John Henry

Entire Class

9 + Readers: NARRATORS 1-4, JOHN, MA, FOREMAN, LITTLE WILLIE, WORKERS (3 OR MORE)

JOHN: MA, I think it's time I struck out on my own.

MA: What are you thinking, John? We've always been farmers, the whole family workin' together.

JOHN, Well, Ma, I've got my heart set on bein' a railroad man.

MA: Fiddlesticks! You belong here drivin' the mules, not a train.

JOHN: Oh, I'm not gonna <u>drive</u> a train. I wanna lay the rails for 'em?

MA: John,…

JOHN: Ma, I told ya. I got my heart set.

NARRATOR 1: So John left the farm in hopes of joining the railroad company.

FOREMAN: Hello, young man. What can I do for you?

JOHN: Well, I'm looking to become part of your crew. Are you hiring?

FOREMAN: Maybe 'n maybe not. What's your experience?

JOHN: Well, none at steel-drivin', but I've been swingin' an axe on the farm since I was a tiny tot.

FOREMAN: We really can't hire a man without experience. It's just too dangerous. If you don't do it just right, your sledgehammer could hurt someone.

JOHN: Sir, my aim is real good. Please give me a chance. I know I could drive that spike over there into the ground with one swing.

FOREMAN: Well, now you've done it! We don't tolerate braggarts on this crew. Go back to the farm.

Workers: *Each jeeringly says any one of these lines. All shout simultaneously.*

No way!

Hey, give him a chance!

Let's see him try!

This I wanna see!

Let him give it a shot!

JOHN: Will someone hold the spike for me?

LITTLE WILLIE: I'd be proud to.

Crew members gasp.

NARRATOR 2: Little Willie held the spike, and the crowd held their breath.

NARRATOR 3: John swung that sledgehammer with all his might and drove the spike deep into the ground.

NARRATOR 4: The foreman and crew members were dead silent for a full minute. Then they broke into cheers.

WORKERS: *Each says any one of theses lines. All shout simultaneously.*

Unbelievable!

All right!

Wow!

Good job!

NARRATOR 5: When silence returned, the foreman spoke.

FOREMAN: I'd be proud to have you on my crew.

JOHN: I'd be proud to be one of you.

Crew members cheer.

NARRATOR 1: For months, John worked hard, and everyone on the crew liked him.

NARRATOR 2: Then one day a salesman arrived at the camp.

SALESMAN: Where can I find your foreman?

FOREMAN: I'm the foreman. What can I do for you?

SALESMAN: I'm here to tell you what I can do for you. How would you like to buy an invention that will get your work done in one-tenth the time?

FOREMAN: What?

SALESMAN: Here's a picture of it. It's called a steam drill.

FOREMAN: And it does what?

SALESMAN: It'll break a tunnel through a mountain in no time. It can drive a drill faster than any man alive can swing a hammer!

FOREMAN: I don't need any newfangled machine. I've got John Henry.

SALESMAN: You think your man is stronger than this steam drill?

FOREMAN: Yep.

SALESMAN: Would you like to wager on that? If your man can beat my steam drill, I'll give it to you FREE! If my steam drill beats your man, you'll buy the steam drill.

FOREMAN: It's a deal.

NARRATOR 3: News of the contest spread like wild fire.

NARRATOR 4: People from miles around gathered the next day to watch.

NARRATOR 1: At 7:00 A.M. the town mayor stood ready to start the contest.

NARRATOR 2: Before he could speak, a roar went up from the men on John's crew.

WORKERS: *Each says any one of these lines. All shout simultaneously, repeating until mayor interrupts.*

Go for it, John!
You show 'em, John!
Hip-hip-hooray for John!
We're all behind you, boy!
MAYOR: *Interrupting to silence the crowd.*
Gentlemen, when I blow the whistle, you will have exactly four hours. When I blow the whistle at the end of the four hours, whoever has dug the farthest into the rock will be the winner. Ready?
Mayor blows whistle.

NARRATOR 2: For two hours John Henry and the man with the steam drill pounded away at the rock. Then Little Willlie went over and wiped the sweat from John's brow.
LITTLE WILLIE: John, how are you feeling?
JOHN: Fit as can be. How's the steam drill doing?
LITTLE WILLIE: Well, it's a bit ahead of you, but not by much.
JOHN: I'll catch him.
LITTLE WILLIE: I know you will, John.
NARRATOR 3: Another two hours passed, and Willie was worried about his friend.
LITTLE WILLIE: John, do you wanna take a rest?
JOHN: Why? I'm doing fine.
LITTLE WILLIE: The steam drill has a broken bit. It's gonna take that guy some time to fix it. You might as well take a breather.
JOHN: Nope. I've gotta keep at it. In fact, bring me another hammer. I can use two at a time.
NARRATOR 4: And he did.
NARRATOR 1: Soon the drill bit was replaced and the hammering continued until…
Mayor blows whistle
MAYOR: Mr. Victors, will you please measure the depth of each hole?
Pause
MR. VICTORS: John Henry's hole is deeper by four feet.
Workers cheer loudly!
Pause
NARRATOR 4: John Henry didn't hear the cheering of the crowd.
NARRATOR 3: His heart had burst.

NARRATOR 2: He lay beside the chips of rock with two hammers still in his hands.

NARRATOR 1: They buried him beside the railroad tracks.

NARRATOR 2: To this day, whenever a train passes his grave, the engineer blows his whistle as if to say:

ALL EXCEPT JOHN: HERE LIES A STEEL-DRIVIN' MAN!

Liberty or Death
by Patrick Henry
6 Readers: READER 1,2,3,4; HENRY 1,2

Prologue

READER 1: Patrick Henry, a leading Virginia lawyer,
READER 2: a fiery orator, a legislator,
READER 3: a staunch advocate of political liberty.
READER 4: He gave this speech before the Virginia Convention of 1776.
READER 2: It was a call to action.
READER 3: It was a call for liberty or death.
READER 1: His words and ideals are herein presented
READER 4: with our help and interpretation.

Address

HENRY 1: Mr. President, no man thinks more highly that I do of patriotism.
HENRY 2: But different men often see the same objects in different lights.
HENRY 1: I hope that it will not be thought disrespectful to those gentlemen,
HENRY 2: to entertain opinions of a character very opposite to theirs.
HENRY 1: I speak forth my sentiments freely and without reserve.
READER 1: This is the time for frankness.
READER 2: Speak on.
HENRY 1: It is a question of freedom or slavery.
HENRY 2: The subject is the debate of freedom.
READER 3: Speak your mind.
READER 4: It is the only way we can arrive at truth.
HENRY 1: Shall I hold back my opinions at such a time?
READER 4: Fulfill your great responsibility!
HENRY 2: Shall I fear giving offense?
READER 1: You would be guilty of treason if you give in to your fears.
HENRY 1: Shall I revere all earthly kings?
READER 2: You would be disloyal toward the majesty of heaven.
HENRY 2: Mr. President, we are apt to shut our eyes against a painful truth,
HENRY 1: and to listen to the song of that siren,
HENRY 2: till she transforms us into beasts.
READER 1: This is not the part of wise men,

READER 2: engaged in a great and arduous struggle for liberty.

READER 3: Are we disposed to be of that number

READER 4: who have eyes but see not,

READER 2: who have ears, but hear not.

HENRY 1: I am willing to know the whole truth,

HENRY 2: to know the worst and provide for it.

HENRY 1: I have but one lamp by which my feet are guided.

READER 3: That is the lamp of experience.

HENRY 1: I know of no way of judging of the future but by the past.

HENRY 2: The past is an insidious smile of the British ministry.

HENRY 1: The past is a snare for our feet.

HENRY 2: The past is to be betrayed by a kiss.

HENRY 1: The past is fleets and armies.

READER 4: Is this British love and reconciliation?

READER 3: Is this the British way to win back our love?

HENRY 1: No, these are implements of war and subjugation.

HENRY 2: What means this martial array?

READER 3: Its purpose is to force us.

HENRY 2: Has Great Britain any enemy in this quarter of the world

HENRY 1: to call for all this accumulation of navies and armies?

READER 1: No, she has none.

READER 2: Then, they are meant for us!

HENRY 2: What have we to oppose them?

READER 3: Arguments. Talk.

HENRY 2: We have been trying this for ten years.

HENRY 1: Have we anything new to offer on the subject?

READER 1: Nothing.

HENRY 1: Shall we resort to entreaty and humble supplications?

READER 2: It has all been in vain.

READER 4: Deceive yourselves no longer.

HENRY 2: We have done everything that could be done

HENRY 1: to avert the storm which is now coming on.

READER 1: Petitioned.

READER 2: Remonstrated.

READER 3: Supplicated.

READER 4: And prostrated ourselves before the tyrannical hands of the Parliament.

HENRY 1: Our petitions have been slighted.

HENRY 2: Our remonstrance have produced violence and insult.
HENRY 1: Our supplications have been spurned.
HENRY 2: Our prostrations have been held in contempt by the throne itself.
HENRY 1: We have indulged in the fond hope of peace and reconciliation.
HENRY 2: Is there no longer any room for hope?
HENRY 1: If we wish to be free,
HENRY 2: if we wish to preserve inviolate those inestimable privileges
HENRY 1: for which we have been so long contending, then we must fight?
ALL READERS: We must fight!
READER 4: We need to appeal to arms.
READER 1: O God of Hosts hear our appeal!
READER 4: They tell us that we are weak.
READER 1: When shall we be stronger?
READER 4: Next week or next year?
READER 1: When we are totally disarmed?
READER 4: When a British guard shall be stationed in every house?
HENRY 1: We are not weak.
HENRY 2: We will act!
HENRY 1: We have the power from the God of nature.
READER 2: Three millions of people,
READER 3: armed in the holy cause of liberty,
READER 2: and in such a country as that which we posses,
READER 3: are invincible by any force which our enemy can send against us.
HENRY 2: We shall not fight our battles alone.
HENRY 1: There is a just God
HENRY 2: who presides over the destinies of nations
HENRY 1: and who will raise friends to fight our battles for us.
READER 1: Are we strong enough for the battle?
HENRY 1: The battle is not to the strong alone.
HENRY 2: The battle is to the vigilant,
HENRY 1: the active,
HENRY 2: the brave.
READER 2: Is it too late to retire from the contest?
HENRY 1: There is no retreat but in submission and slavery!
HENRY 2: Our chains are forged!
HENRY 1: The war is inevitable.
HENRY 2: Let it come.
ALL READERS: Let the war come?

Reader 2: But what of peace?

ALL READERS: We want peace.

HENRY 1: There is no peace.

HENRY 2: The war is actually begun!

HENRY 1: Our brethren are already in the field!

HENRY 2: Is life so dear or peace so sweet,

HENRY 1: as to be purchased at the price of chains and slavery?

ALL READERS: Forbid it, Almighty God!

HENRY 2: Why stand we here idle?

READER 4: What is your wish?

READER 3: What would you have us do?

HENRY 1: I know not what course others may take,

HENRY 2: but as for me,

HENRY 1: Give me liberty,

HENRY 2: or give me death.

ALL READERS: Give us liberty!

Old Rat's Tale

Readers 7: Voice s 1-6 and Audience (Entire Class)

VOICE 1: This is a tale.

VOICE 2: A story tale,

VOICE 4: or a wiggly tail?

VOICE 1: Both.

AUDIENCE: Both?

VOICE 3: How can this be?

VOICE 1: It's a story.

VOICE 2: Aha! A story tale—t-a-l-e.

VOICE 1: Well, yes, but, it's about my fellow rats.

VOICE 5: Aha! With wiggly tails—t-a-i-l-s.

VOICE 1: Yes, with wiggly tails of which they were very proud, but…

AUDIENCE: but what?!

VOICE 1: I'm not sure I can talk about it.

AUDIENCE: Why not?

VOICE 1: Because it's so sad.

VOICE 2: Why?

AUDIENCE: Yes, tell us.

VOICE 1: Well, sob, I'll try

VOICE 6: **AN OLD RAT'S TALE**

VOICE 1: He was a rat

VOICE 4: and she was a rat

VOICE 6: And down in one hole they did dwell.

VOICE 4: And both were as black

VOICE 5: as a witch's cat,

VOICES 1,4: and they loved each other well.

VOICE 1: He had a tail

VOICE 4: and she had a tail,

VOICE 6: both long and curly and fine.

VOICE 5: And each said,

VOICE 4: Yours is the finest tail, except, of course, for mine!

VOICE 1: He smelled the cheese,

VOICE 4: and she smelled the cheese,

VOICE 6: And they both pronounced it good.

VOICE 5: And they both remarked it would greatly add

VOICE 6: to the charm of their daily food.

VOICE 1: So he ventured out,
VOICE 4: and she ventured out,
VOICE 1: And I watched them in great pain!
VOICE 6: 'Cause what befell them
VOICE 1: I'll never tell————-for they never came back again.
AUDIENCE: Boohoo, Boohoo!

Susanna from the Hebrew Tradition

7 Readers: READER 1, 2, 3; ELDER 1, 2; SUSANNA, DANIEL

READER 1: Susanna was very beautiful.

READER 2: She feared the Lord,

READER 3: had righteous parents,

READER 2: was taught according to the law of Moses.

READER 1: She was married to a very rich man,

READER 3: who was most honored.

READER 1: Many Jews came to his large house

READER 2: and to his spacious garden.

READER 1: In that year two Elders from Babylon were appointed as judges.

READER 3: The two Elders from Babylon

READER 2: were frequently at Susanna's house,

READER 1: to decide on the lawsuits.

READER 3: At noon Susanna would go into her husband's garden to walk.

READER 2: The two evil Elders from Babylon were there every day

READER 1: watching her walk,

READER 2: watching her talk

READER 3: and desiring her.

READER 1: Both were overwhelmed with passion.

READER 3: Susanna was very beautiful.

READER 2: They did not tell one another of their lust.

READER 1: They waited eagerly day after day to see her.

READER 3: One day the two Elders said,

ELDER 1 & 2: let us go home, for it is mealtime.

READER 1 They parted from each other

READER 3: but came back to the garden from different ways,

ELDER 1: Why are you going back?

ELDER 2: Why are you going back?

READER 2: They finally confessed their lust

READER 1: and arranged a time when both could find her alone.

READER 2: Then the opportune time came.

READER 3: Susanna wished a bath in the garden, for it was very hot.

READER 2: She spoke to her two maids.

SUSANNA: Shut the garden gates so that I may bathe.

READER 3: The maids shut the garden gates and left the garden.

READER 2: Susanna thought she was alone in the garden,

READER 1: but was surprised to see and hear the two elders.

ELDER 1: Look, the garden doors are shut.

ELDER 2: We are alone, no one sees us.

ELDERS 1 & 2: We are in love with you.

ELDER 1: Come and lie with us.

SUSANNA: I am hemmed in. If I do it, it is death.

ELDER 2: If you refuse we will say

ELDER 1: that a young man was with you

ELDER 2: and that is the reason that you sent your maids away.

SUSANNA: If I don't do it, I will not escape your hand.

ELDER 1: Come and lie with us.

SUSANNA: No! I will not lie with you. I will not sin in the sight of the Lord.

READER 2: Then Susanna cried out with a loud voice.

SUSANNA: Help, help!

READER 1: The two Elders shouted against her

READER 2: and one ran and opened the garden gate.

READER 3: Then the servants rushed in at the side door

READER 2: to see what had happened to her.

READER 1: They were greatly ashamed

READER 2: when they heard the Elders tell their false tale.

READER 3: The next day when all the people gathered at the house of her husband two Elders came.

ELDERS 1 & 2: Send for Susanna.

READER 1: So Susanna came

READER 2: with her parents,

READER 1: with her children,

READER 3: with her kindred,

READER 1: with her beauty,

READER 2: with her refinement,

READER 3: with her veil.

ELDER 2: Take off the veil!

READER 2: Her family wept.

READER 1: Her friends wept.

READER 2: Susanna wept as she said,

SUSANNA: I have done no evil.

READER 3:Here is the story of the two elders.

ELDER 1: As we were walking in the garden

ELDER 2: this woman came in with two maids,

ELDER 1: shut the garden doors and dismissed the maids.

ELDER 2: A young man who had been hidden

ELDER 2: came to her and lay with her.

ELDER 1: We were in the corner of the garden

ELDER 2: and, when we saw this wickedness,

ELDER 1: we ran to them.

ELDER 2: We could not hold the man

ELDER 1: for he was too strong for us.

ELDER 2: So we seized this young woman

ELDER 1: and asked her who the young man was,

ELDER 2: but she did not know.

READER 2: The assembly believed them!

READER 1: She was condemned to death

READER 3: in spite of her words of defense:

SUSANNA: O, eternal God who does discern what is secret,
who is aware of all things before they come to be.
You know that these men have borne false witness against me.
And now I am to die! I have done none of these things.
They have invented wickedness against me.

READER 3: Just as they were about to take her out to be killed,

READER 1: a voice spoke out,

DANIEL: Have you condemned a daughter of Israel without an examination?

READER 2: It was Daniel speaking.

DANIEL: Have you condemned a daughter of Israel without the facts?

READER 1: Daniel was forceful in his words.

DANIEL: These men have borne false witness against her.

READER 3: His words and presence commanded respect.

DANIEL: Separate the two Elders far from each other. I will examine them.

READER 2: The elders were separated and Daniel began his examination of the first Elder.

DANIEL: Under which tree did you see her being intimate?

ELDER 2: Under a mastic tree.

READER 2: The other Elder was brought in and asked,

Daniel: Under which tree did you see her being intimate?

Elder 1: Under an evergreen oak.

DANIEL: Very well, you both lied against your own heads. The angel of God has received the sentence from God and will immediately cut you in two.

READER 2: And they rose against the Elders

READER 1: and they did to them as they had
READER 2: wickedly planned to do to Susanna.
READER 1: They put them to death in accordance with the law of Moses.
READER 2: And so the question can be asked today, in fact, especially today,
READER 3: if there is no justice for women,
READER 2: can there be justice for anyone?

There's Only One 'I'

16 Readers

VOICES 1-11: There's only one "I" in all creation.
VOICE 12: There's only one "I" in our nation.
VOICE 13: There's only one "I" in our whole universe.
VOICES 1-11: There's only one "I" in all creation.

VOICE 14: There's only one "I" in our community.
VOICE 15: There's only one "I" in our great city.
VOICE 16: There's only one "I" in the United States.
VOICES 1-11: There's only one "I" in all creation.

VOICES 1-11: There's only one "I" in all creation.
VOICE 12: There's only one "I" in our nation.
VOICE 13: There's only one "I" in our whole universe.
VOICES 1-11: There's only one "I" in all creation.
ALL: I must be responsible!

These Things Called Maps
4 Readers

READER 1: Maps tell us north from south,

READER 2: east from west,

READER 3: up from down.

READER 4: Maps tell us how far, how long,

READER 2: how big, how high, how many.

READER 1: Maps tell us where to go,

READER 3: how to go,

READER 2: but not when to go!

READER 4: Maps lead us, guide us, protect us.

READER 2: This is a poem about a map that shows heights, and depths,

READER 1: and seas, and sands,

READER 3: and pinnacles, and mire,

READER 4: and paths and Heaven.

READER 2: Oh, pray, kind sir,

READER 1: Do you have a map that shows the heights of fame,

READER 4: the sea of doubt, the depths of fear?

READER 3: Or, do you have a map on which will show

READER 2: from whence the north winds came,

READER 1: the sands of time and the pinnacles of success,

READER 3: the mire of despair, the road to ruin,

READER 4: and the path of righteousness?

READER 3: It should show

READER 2: the trail to yesteryear

READER 1: and to Heaven, where good folks go.

READER 3: Pray tell me, kind sir,

READER 2: have you such a map?

READER 4: For truly I want to know.

Three Billy Goats Gruff

READERS 1 & 2; LITTLE GOAT, MIDDLE GOAT, BIG GOAT, SOUND-MAKERS, AUDIENCE

READER 1: The Three Billy Goats Gruff.

READER 2: Once upon a time,

READER 1: there were three billy goats.

LITTLE GOAT: I am Little Goat.

MIDDLE GOAT: I am Middle Goat.

BIG GOAT: I am Big Goat.

MIDDLE GOAT: We had eaten all the grass in the field,

LITTLE GOAT: and we were hungry.

MIDDLE GOAT: We could see green grass

LITTLE GOAT: on the other side of the river

BIG GOAT: so we wanted to cross the bridge.

READER 2: Little Goat started across the bridge.

SOUND-MAKERS: Trip, trap, trip, trap, trip, trap.

READER 1: Suddenly a troll came up out of the water.

READER 2: He roared,

AUDIENCE: Who's that trip-trapping on my bridge!?

LITTLE GOAT: It is I, Little Goat.

AUDIENCE: Get off my bridge or I will eat you!

LITTLE GOAT: Oh, please do not eat me. My bigger brother is coming. You will like him better.

READER 2: The troll growled.

AUDIENCE: GRRRRRRR!

READER 1: But he let Little Goat pass over the bridge.

SOUND-MAKERS: Trip, trap, trip, trap, trip, trap.

READER 1: Next Middle Goat started across the bridge.

SOUND-MAKERS: **Trip, trap, trip, trap, trip, trap.**

READER 2: Suddenly the troll came up out of the water.

AUDIENCE: Who's that trip-trapping on my bridge!?

MIDDLE GOAT: It is I, Middle Goat.

AUDIENCE: Get off my bridge or I will eat you!

LITTLE GOAT: Oh, please do not eat me. My bigger brother is coming. You will like him better.

READER 2: The troll growled.

AUDIENCE: GRRRRRRR!

READER 1: But he let Middle Goat pass over the bridge.
SOUND-MAKERS: **Trip, trap, trip, trap, trip, trap.**
READER 2: Big Goat started across the bridge.
SOUND-MAKERS: **TRIP, TRAP, TRIP, TRAP, TRIP, TRAP.**
READER 1: Suddenly the troll came up out of the water.
AUDIENCE: Who's that trip-trapping on my bridge!?
Big Goat: It is I, Big Goat!
Audience: Get off my bridge or I will eat you!
Big Goat: This bridge is not yours.
Little Goat: It belongs to everyone.
Big Goat: Let me pass or I will bump you back in the water.
Middle Goat: And his horns are meaner than your growl!
Reader 2: Big Goat put his head down.
Reader 1: But before he could move,
Reader 2: the troll disappeared into the river.
Readers 1 & 2: From that day on, anyone could cross the bridge.
Sound-makers: **TRIP, TRAP, TRIP, TRAP, TRIP, TRAP.**

Presentational End Notes

- Annie Oakley—Assign parts in advance to ensure a smooth performance. In one classroom with a rather large number of English language learners (ELLs), we assigned an ELL as an understudy for each part and provided practice time for both the performers and their understudies. After the first presentation, the understudies practiced their roles, while all other students worked in three cooperative groups to write their own scripts about other Wild West legendary characters. During the next four days there was a performance a day; the last was a fluent reading of this script by the ELLs, who received the biggest applause of any!

- Boy Who Cried Wolf—Assign the individual roles in advance so students have time to practice fluent reading, using the expression cues. Distribute copies of the script to the entire class. Be prepared to do this brief reading several times with the same casting to get the pacing "just right."

  A follow-up discussion about scare tactics in current events can be very effective in making the moral of this fable relevant to today's world.

- Call 911—This short script can be repeated throughout the unit. Advanced readers are assigned the individual roles for the initial reading. Over time all students get to be soloists. Even struggling readers can read with expression because of the repeated exposure to the text.

- Colonist and Tea Time—Assign the six roles to advanced readers. Allow them time to practice using their voices expressively. This will arouse the audience's interest during this introduction to the causes of the Revolutionary War. After the presentation class members can question, even argue with the characters. What a dynamic way to start a history unit!

- Columbus' Press Conference—This script can certainly be read in the traditional manner, with four solo readers. To engage all students, however, the teacher may choose to select three students to read the reporters' lines and ask the entire class to read Columbus' lines chorally. Comparing the information in this RT with textbook facts can make an interesting, and hopefully unforgettable, lesson.

- Gettysburg Address Prologue—Select two readers to present; or, as the instructor, read the part of Reader 1 while the entire class reads the Reader 2 part in unison.

- Gettysburg Address—Having students practice this reading before presentation will help all to appreciate and internalize Lincoln's important words.

- Good Morning Mr. President—Arrange the class into two groups, per the directions at the top of the script. Highlighting the lines on individual scripts and lining students up in order on the two sides prepares for a smooth performance. "Extras" should be at the end of each line of reporters; they should also have highlighted scripts and be reminded that the choral lines on which they join in have the most emotional impact of any. To add interest, the teacher may pass a microphone from speaker to speaker. This will also make obvious each shift across the centuries.

- Hangin' Chad—Select four students to practice and read for the class. As a follow-up students should be drawn into discussion, leading them to realize susequent impact of this event, for instance, that the date of the California gubernatorial recall election in 2003 was contested over voting machines that still could produce hanging chads.

- I Have A Dream—Assign roles and allow time for practice so the presentation is fluent and expressive. Students acting with their voices help the audience internalize the message of this powerful speech by Dr. King. The reading, which is rather long, is divided into six sections. The teacher may opt to use only a portion of the reading to fit the lesson of the day. Biographies, proclamations, and historic speeches can be used to explore the lives of famous individuals, foster positive attitudes, and teach the significant concepts within historical developments. Once students have performed the "I Have a Dream" RT, they may choose to prepare their own scripts based on the lives and works of other historical figures.

- John Henry—Assign parts, adding as many workers as necessary to ensure that all students have lines to read. In this case, the workers actually serve as the audience, since they are the bystanders in the scenes.

As a follow-up, students may analyze the script, identifying the facts and the exaggerations within this legend.

- Liberty or Death—This reading is best given by six readers who have had an opportunity to practice carefully. The class can be divided into four or five groups to make presentations. Students eagerly listen to multiple readings, noting differences in interpretations. As students listen to each other's performances of this script, they can identify ways the readers have used their voices to show various emotions and attitudes: hardness, sarcasm, superiority, innocence, doubt, pride, defiance, irritability, joy, anger, etc. This will prepare students to label their own voicing directions.

- Old Rat's Tale—Since the audience is involved in this reading, a copy is needed for at least every two students of the audience. If duplication poses a problem, make one transparency of the script to be projected and just enough copies for the main readers. As a follow-up language arts activity, students may hunt for homophones within the script.

- There's Only One 'I'—Cards are prepared with the following words and letters:

NATION, UNIVERSE, COMMUNITY, CITY, THE UNITED STATES, A, L, L, C, R, E, A, T, I, O, N.

Wherever an "I" appears it is printed in red; all other letters are black.

If there are more than 16 students, two or three students may hold a given word card and share the matching line(s).

Students holding the letter cards to form "ALL CREATION" stand in the back row. Those holding word cards sit in the front.

As a follow-up, students make commitments to take personal responsibility for some social or environmental action.

For a performance of this script by third graders, we set the text to music. The children wore white shirts and red ties. As they sang their lines they raised their cards. They then shared their personal promises to better their world. The guests in the audience were duly impressed!

- Susanna—This reading has a tremendous impact if well practiced before presentation. It stimulates discussion of modern-day issues related to women's rights.

- These Things Called Maps—Select four individuals to practice reading before the presentation.

  As a follow-up, ask the students to divide the script into two parts: the literal description of a map's functions and the metaphorical description of life's journeys.

- Three Billy Goats Gruff—

  Assign roles, noting that the sound-makers have the least demanding, but the most interesting part. Following the performance, students discuss an historical event, pre-selected by the teacher. They equate specific actions with the goats' and troll's behaviors. As an extension, students can read other versions of this tale and see how they parallel different power struggles within history.

  In one class, students compared the goats to African-Americans in the Deep South, who pleaded and demonstrated, until they finally won the right to patronize the same restaurants and attend the same schools as whites.

Reference List

Coger, L., and White, M. (1982) <u>Readers Theatre Handbook: A dramatic Approach to Literature</u>. 3rd Edition. Glenview, IL, Scott Foresman.

Caine, G. and Caine, R. (1991). <u>Making Connections</u>. Alexandria, Va: ASCD.s

Gardner, H. (1983). <u>Frames of Mind.</u> New York: Basic Books.

Hecklemann, R. G. (1969). <u>Neurological impress method of remedial reading instruction</u>. Academic Therapy Quarterly, Volume 4, pp. 277-282.

Martinez, M., Roser, N. and Strecker, S. (1998-1999) "I never thought I could be a star": A readers theatre ticket to fluency. <u>The Reading Teacher</u>, 52, 326-334.

Prescott, J. (2003) The power of reader's theater. <u>Instructor.</u> January/February, pp 22-28.

Roy, D. (2000) personal communications.

Bibliography

The following list includes books that lend themselves particularly well to Readers Theatre. Note "and above" after each elementary grade range. Many books considered "children's books" have surface messages children enjoy, but also much deeper messages only older students can truly understand. Revisiting childhood favorites through a Readers Theatre format, which requires voice interpretation, is often a powerful experience for more mature students.

GRADES K-4 AND ABOVE

Aardema. V. (1981). Bringing the Rain to Kapiti Plain. New York: Penguin Books.

Brown, M. (1949). The Important Book. New York: Harper Row.

Brown, R. (1991). The World that Jack Built. New York: Dutton Children's Books.

Cannon, J. (1993). Stellaluna. San Diego: Harcourt, Brace.

Carle, E. (1990). The Very Quiet Cricket. New York: Putman & Grosset.

Charlip, R. (1964). Fortunately. New York: Simon & Schuster.

Cherry, L. (1990). The Great Kapok Tree. New York: Harcourt Brace Jovanovich.

Dotlich, R. (2003). In the Spin of Things. Honesville, PA: Boyd Mills Press.

Faulkner, K (1996). The Wide-mouthed Frog. New York: Dial Books.

Fleishman, P. (1989). I am Phoenix: Poems for Two Voices. New York: HarperCollins.

Fleishman, P. (1992). Joyful Noise: Poems for Two Voices. New York: HarperCollins.

Fleming, D. (1992). Lunch. New York: Henry Holt and Company.

Geisel, T. (1961). The Star-bellied Sneetches. New York: Random House.

Geisel, T. (1971). The Lorax. New York: Random House.

Gilman, P. (1992). Something from Nothing. New York: Scholastic.

Greenfield, E. (1978). "Harriet Tubman." In Honey, I Love. Harper Collins Publishers.

Hutchins, P. (1986). The Doorbell Rang. New York: Greenwillow Books.

Kasca, K. (1987). The Wolf's Chicken Stew. New York: Putnam & Grosset.

Kellogg, S. (1989). Is Your Mama a Llama? New York: Scholastic.

Lowell, S. (1994). The Tortoise and the Jackrabbit. Flagstaff, AZ: Northland Publishing.

Lyon, G. (1989). Together. New York: Orchard Books.

Marsh, T. and Ward, J. (1998). Way out in the Desert. Flagstaff, AZ: Northland.

Mayer, M. I Was So Mad. New York: Golden Books.

McGovern, A. (1965). Stone Soup. New York: Scholastic.

McLerran, A. (1991) Roxaboxen. New York: Scholastic

Munsch, R. (1980). The Paperbag Princess. Willowdale, Ont., Canada: Firefly Books.

Numeroff, L. (1991). If You Give a Moose a Muffin. New York: Harper Collins

Peet, B. (1973). <u>The Spooky Tail of Prewitt Peacock.</u> New York: Houghton Mifflin.

Pfister, M. (1992). <u>The Rainbow Fish.</u> New York: North-South Books.

Philpot, L. & G. (1993). <u>Amazing Anthony Ant.</u> New York: Random House.

Poe, M. & Schmitt, B. (1987). Selected poems from <u>Finnigin and Friends</u>. North Billerica, MA: Curriculum Associates.

Poe, M. & Schmitt, B. (1987). Selected poems from <u>Willie MacGurkle</u>. North Billerica, MA: Curriculum Associates.

Root, P. (1998). <u>One Duck Stuck.</u> Cambridge, MA: Candlewick Press.

Rylant, C. (1982). <u>When I was Young in the Mountains.</u> New York: Dutton.

Scieszka, J. (1989). <u>The True Story of the Three Little Pigs.</u> New York: Penguin Books.

Seeger, P. (1963). <u>Abiyoyo.</u> New York: Scholastic.

Soto, G. (1996). <u>The Old Man & His Door.</u> New York: Putnam's Sons.

Wood, A. (1984). <u>The Napping House.</u> New York: Harcourt Brace Jovanovich.

Young, E. (1992). <u>Seven Blind Mice.</u> New York: Scholastic.

GRADES 5-8 AND ABOVE

Fox, M. (1989). <u>Feather and Fools.</u> San Diego, CA: Harcourt Brace & Company.

Fox, M. (1985). <u>Wilfrid Gordon McDonald Partridge.</u> Brooklyn, NY: Kane/Miller Book Publishers.

Hayes, J. (1993). <u>Soft Child.</u> Tucson, AZ: Harbinger House.

Lyon, G. (1992). <u>Who Came Down the Road?</u> New York: Orchard Books.

Wood, D. (1992). <u>Old Turtle.</u> Duluth, MN: Pfiefer-Hamilton.

HIGH SCHOOL AND ADULT

Bunting, E. (1991). <u>Fly Away Home.</u> New York: Houghton Mifflin.

Canfield, J. and Hansen, M. (1993). <u>Chicken Soup for the Soul</u>. Deerfield Beach, FL: Health Communications.

Climo, S. (1993). <u>The Korean Cinderella.</u> New York: Harper and Row.

Costanzo, C. (1999). <u>The Twelve Gifts of Birth.</u> Phoenix, AZ: Featherfew.

Frost, R. (1969). <u>Stopping by Woods on a Snowy Evening.</u> New York: Dutton Childrens Books.

Lawson, H. (1970). <u>The Loaded Dog.</u> North Ryde, NSW: Angus & Robertson.

Martin, R. (1992). <u>The Rough-Face Girl.</u> New York: G.P. Putnam's Sons.

Munsch, R. (1986). <u>Love You Forever.</u> Willowdale, Ont., Canada: Firefly Books.

Parker, K. (1970). <u>Tales of Dreamtime.</u> North Ryde, NSW: Angus & Robertson.

Paterson, A. (1990). <u>A Vision Splendid.</u> North Ryde, NSW: Angus & Robertson.

Pollock, P. (1996). <u>The Turkey Girl.</u> Boston: Little, Brown and Company.

Schroeder, A. (1997). <u>Smoky Mountain Rose.</u> New York: Dial Books.

Silverstein, S. (1974). <u>Where the Sidewalk Ends.</u> New York: Harper and Row.

Silverstein, S. (1981). <u>A Light in the Attic.</u> New York: Harper and Row.

Silverstein, S. (1996). <u>Falling Up.</u> New York: Harper and Row.

BOOKS AND ARTICLES ABOUT READERS THEATRE

Barchers, S. (1993). Readers Theatre for Beginning Readers. Englewood, CO: Teacher Ideas Press.

Braun, W. and Braun, C. (January 2000). A Readers Theatre Treasury of Stories. Winnipeg, MA, Canada: Portage and Main Press

Campbell, M. (Summer, 1993). Readers theatre a unique way to teach reading, Journal of Adventist Education.

Campbell, M. and Zackrison, E. (July/August,1994). Responsive reading and scripture readings, Worship Leader, pp 19-26, 35.

Fredericks, A. (April 2001). Readers Theatre for American History. Englewood, CO: Teacher Ideas Press.

Fredericks, A. (December 1993). Frantic Frogs and Other Frankly Fractured Folktales for Readers Theatre. Englewood, CO: Teacher Ideas Press.

Latrobe, K., Casey C., Gann, L. (1991). Social Studies Readers Theatre for Young Adults. Englewood, CO: Teacher Ideas Press.

Laughlin, M. and Latrobe, K. (1990). Readers Theatre for Children. Englewood, CO: Teacher Ideas Press.

McClay, J. (1971). Readers Theatre: Toward a Grammar of Practice, New York, Random house, Inc.

Neill Dixon, N. et al (April 1996). Learning With Readers Theatre: Building Connections. Winnipeg, MA, Canada: Peguis Pub Ltd.

Ratliff, G. (1999). Introduction to Readers Theatre, A Guide to Classroom Performance. Colorado Springs, CO: Meriwether Publishing.

Robertson, M. and Poston-Anderson, B. (1986). Readers Theatre: A Practical Guide. Sydney: Hodder and Stoughton.

Swanson, C. (1998). Reading and Writing Readers Theatre Scripts, Australian Reading Association, Reading Around: Series Number One, PO Box 589, Wagga Wagga, NSW, March.

Walker, L. (1996). <u>Readers Theatre in the Middle school and Junior High Classroom.</u> Colorado Springs, CO: Meriwether Publishing.

White, M.(1993). <u>Readers Theatre Anthology.</u> Colorado Springs, CO: Meriwether Publishing.

WEB SITES

http://scriptsforschools.com/
More than 150 scripts can be purchased from their catalog.

http://www.aaronshep.com/rt/
Provides free scripts for young readers and an online guide to Readers Theatre scripting, staging, and performing. The site gives information on good books for Readers Theatre.

http://www.qesn.meq.gouv.qc.ca/schools/bchs/rtheatre/
Discusses how Readers Theatre is used by Baie Comeau High School.
Scripts written by the students at Baie Comeau High School can be downloaded. Resources are given to help English and Language Arts classes find more scripts.

http://mirror.eschina.bnu.edu.cn/Mirror1/accesseric/www.indiana.edu/
 eric_rec/ieo/bibs/rdr-thea.html
Provides a bibliography of the literature on Readers Theatre with a focus on use in elementary school. Many references are made to the ERIC Clearinghouse.

http://teachingheart.net/readerstheater.htm
Great site for free Readers Theatre for elementary classroom use.

About the Authors

Campbell and Cleland first met at the International Reading Association Convention in Auckland, New Zealand. Since that time they have been pouring their classroom experience, ideas, and Readers Theatre scripts into this book. In addition to their vast experience in the classroom using Readers Theatre they have successfully used the scripts on their grandchildren, who grace both of their homes.

Campbell and Cleland have earned doctorates in chemistry and reading education respectively. Both have taught on all levels of education. They have spent their professional lives teaching teachers to teach science and reading. While their academic backgrounds are poles apart they have merged the best of their experiences for creative and exciting way to teach students fluency, love of reading, and subject content.

Mel Campbell can often be found in classrooms in southern California developing fluency in students through the use of his Readers Theatre scripts. His most recent appointment was Professor of Curriculum and Instruction at La Sierra University. He lives in Riverside, CA with his wife and his 3000 plus road map collection. When he isn't writing RT, he is out flying his 2 and 4 string kites and birding with his wife. He holds a doctorate from Purdue University and a master's from University of Tennessee.

Jo Cleland, a teacher's teacher, has a special passion for preparing Readers Theatre scripts. She worked in the public schools as a classroom teacher and reading specialist for 21 years, and at Arizona State University West as an education professor for 12 years. She holds a doctorate in curriculum and instruction and master's degree in reading education from Northern Arizona University. Jo is also a professional cellist, who plays with the Symphony of the West Valley. She lives with her husband of 44 years in Phoenix, AZ.

Many teachers have profited from the authors' expertise, through their writings, lectures, seminars and presentations at professional meetings.

0-595-30440-0

Printed in the United States
126549LV00001B/297/A